Global Enterprise Transitions:
Managing the Process

Yi-chen Lan
University of Western Sydney, Australia

Bhuvan Unhelkar
University of Western Sydney, Australia

IDEA GROUP PUBLISHING
Hershey • London • Melbourne • Singapore

658.049
£24g

Acquisitions Editor:	Mehdi Khosrow-Pour
Senior Managing Editor:	Jan Travers
Managing Editor:	Amanda Appicello
Development Editor:	Michele Rossi
Copy Editor:	Bernard Kieklak
Typesetter:	Cindy Consonery
Cover Design:	Lisa Tosheff
Printed at:	Yurchak Printing Inc.

Published in the United States of America by
 Idea Group Publishing (an imprint of Idea Group Inc.)
 701 E. Chocolate Avenue
 Hershey PA 17033
 Tel: 717-533-8845
 Fax: 717-533-8661
 E-mail: cust@idea-group.com
 Web site: http://www.idea-group.com

and in the United Kingdom by
 Idea Group Publishing (an imprint of Idea Group Inc.)
 3 Henrietta Street
 Covent Garden
 London WC2E 8LU
 Tel: 44 20 7240 0856
 Fax: 44 20 7379 3313
 Web site: http://www.eurospan.co.uk

MK

Library of Congress Cataloging-in-Publication Data

Lan, Yi-chen, 1969-
 Global enterprise transitions : managing the process / Yi-Chen Lan and Bhuvan
Unhelkar.
    p. cm.
 Summary: "This book discusses the process of transitioning an organization to a global one based
on Information and Communication Technologies (ICT) including careful planning, execution and
monitoring of the organization as it moves into the global market place"--Provided by publisher.
 Includes bibliographical references and index.
 ISBN 1-59140-624-2 (hc) -- ISBN 1-59140-625-0 (sc) -- ISBN 1-59140-626-9 (ebook)
 1. International business enterprises--Management. 2. International business enterprises--
Technological innovations. 3. Information technology--Management. I. Unhelkar, Bhuvan. II.
Title.
 HD62.4.L358 2005
 658'.049--dc22

                                                            2004029768

British Cataloguing in Publication Data
A Cataloguing in Publication record for this book is available from the British Library.
All work contributed to this book is new, previously-unpublished material. The views expressed in
this book are those of the authors, but not necessarily of the publisher.

Dedications

For Anna (YL)

For Amit & Sumit (BU)

Global Enterprise Transitions:
Managing the Process

Table of Contents

Foreword

*"The significant problems we face in life cannot be solved
at the level of thinking at which we created them."*

Albert Einstein

This book is invaluable for businesses at any stage of globalization. During the last few years, this issue of globalization has grown significantly, with businesses examining several options for determining optimal operations and logistics strategies in their attempt to grow and compete in the global marketplace. Due to the complexities involved in innovating and integrating technologies, more often than not the technologies have long been separated from a firm's overall strategic planning. Companies seeking to become global players must pay close attention to and find a delicate balance between globalization, localization, customization, translation and the growing trend towards internationalization. The importance of this book is directly underscored by this ever increasing need to balance business strategies with corresponding technology innovations that provide the underlying impetus for globalizing organizations. The discussions in this book are also extremely valuable to globalizing organizations who need to offset their "late mover disadvantage" in the global arena. For example, when eBay recently entered the European market, it faced an uphill battle with entrenched competitors like QXL in the United Kingdom, Ricardo.de in Germany, iBazaar in France, and Bidlet.com in Sweden. For such large, and also small/medium sized organizations, the processes of globalization outlined in this book, can provide an excellent governing framework.

Due to advances in technology and globalization of markets, organizations have had to improve their internal processes in order to stay competitive. Not only is the speed with which business transactions are being conducting getting faster, but the scope of conducting business is also getting wider. As a result of these evolving changes, organizations are now discovering that improvements to internal processes are not enough. Organizations must therefore get more involved in the management of their supply chain network of all upstream firms that provide the inputs as well as the network of all downstream firms that provide the outputs of the product to the final end customer. Thus, the concept of supply chain, supply chain management (SCM), and now global supply chain management (GSCM) can no longer be defined at a local level and must be defined in terms of a global network of information systems integrated to include both upstream supplier networks and downstream distribution channels. The global methodology basically centers on the need to integrate the various information systems (ERP or otherwise) across the global supply chain to enable quick flow of information between the trading partners. Within the company ERP systems can achieve the desired integration of the information. Inter-company systems can be then linked using EDI/Internet to facilitate the information exchange between companies. Information infrastructure of ERP systems interconnected with the EDI/Internet enable optimal global supply chain strategies.

The key question for businesses to ask is: What will it take for us to be a success in the business environment of tomorrow? Three forces account for most of the convergence of business strategy with organizational structure and information systems. They are rapid innovation of new information technologies, widespread creation of new ideas and concepts about information itself, and extensive development of new information-intensive organizational forms and business strategies. As more countries join the ranks of the industrialized nations, the sophistication of the global market and number of global competitors has eliminated any advantage that organizations had due to their simple presence in international markets. Companies tied to the information economy are typically global right from their inception — the Internet does not permit them to compete in only national markets. At the same time we see massive consolidations of industries from automobiles to banking to pharmaceuticals to cell phones and Internet service providers around the globe. This makes it mandatory for today's international/global/multinational/transnational organization to employ strategic thinking encompassing business processes as well as technological innovations to compete successfully. That is the precise focus of this book, with the authors creating a succinct yet practical understanding of the fundamental processes involved in managing the global enterprise transition based on the context of the firms (i.e., the current conditions of the industry and the firm) in order to generate and sustain a global competitive strategy.

The most agile of global enterprise transition strategies, as discussed in this book, are applicable in any industry and provide an infinite number of value-increasing possibilities for any organization. This executive's guide on global enterprise transition describes what global enterprise transition is, how it is being conducted and managed, and its major opportunities, limitations, issues and risks. It brings together some high quality expository discussions from the authors to identify, define, and explore global enterprise transition methodologies, systems, and processes in order to understand their opportunities, limitations and risks. This is all eventually demonstrated by an example case study from the hospital domain in the last chapter of the book, which adds significant value to the reader's understanding of the theories of the globalization process discussed in all previous chapters.

Organizations need a clearly articulated strategy (i.e., considerations such as central versus distributed control) focusing on taking their organization to a foreign country. This will save the organizations time and expense as they build their global Web presence. A key takeaway is that this book helps the reader identify and understand the facets of various elements/processes that bear on successful entry/exit into/from a country. The authors deserve compliments on writing this scholarly book, and making a significant contribution to the literature in global information systems and related international business disciplines.

Mahesh S. Raisinghani, Ph.D., CEC, CISM

Preface

Purpose of the Book

This book discusses the process of transitioning an organization to a global one. And that transitioning process, based on the latest information and communication technologies (ICT), includes careful planning, execution and monitoring of the organization as it moves into the global market place. While some areas of transitions are discussed in the existing ICT literature, there appears to be a dearth of *practical* coverage of the topic of *managing* global transitions. Furthermore, since most e-transformations are based on electronic technologies, there is a need to discuss the topic of e-transformation as a combination of both business and technology perspectives. In our perusals, we discovered that the current literature on transformations either dealt with the business aspects, or exclusively deals with the technology aspects of the e-transformations. This book brings a synergy between the business and technology aspects of electronic transformations of organizations and aims to address both these crucial aspects of the globalization process. This book outlines the framework for transitioning organizations, how that framework can be applied in practice, and how to understand whether the transition has been successful or not. The technology aspect of transition discussed in this book deals with new technologies such as Web Services that are bringing about a paradigm shift in the process of e-transformations. Finally, the crucial and oft neglected sociological aspect of e-transformation and, more specifically, the change management and human side of transition is also investigated in this book. We hope the readers will find this book a valuable and practical addition to their repertoire of knowledge and literature in electronic transformations of global organizations.

Chapter Summaries

Chapter	Theme	Comments
I	Arguments	This chapter will outline the background reasoning for global enterprise transitions (GET), provide the meaning of globalization and discuss the four eras of global market evolution, highlight organizational transition scopes, and determine the global enterprise transitions roadmap.
II	Vision and Structure	This chapter will discuss the global strategic vision that would encourage the process of globalization within an organization, the global organizational structures and the relating enterprise characteristics.
III	Framework	This chapter will identify and develop the systems and processes framework for global enterprise transition, and investigate the global transition factors in six perspectives including business, human resources, end-user, cultural, environmental and technology.
IV	Enactment	This chapter will discusses the practical enactment of the Global Enterprise Transition process and the corresponding activities involved in enactment of the global enterprise transitions.
V	Technology	This chapter deals with the underlying technologies for globalization – more specifically those of Web Services.
VI	Case study	This is an example case study demonstrating the practical aspect of globalizing an organization; a hospital has been considered for this purpose.

Readership

This book will be of primary interest to two reader categories:

1) The strategic decision makers in the industry who are involved in the process of electronic transformation of their businesses, particularly those involved in initiating the process; and

2) The researchers and higher degree students of this fascinating subject. These categories are further explained below.

Decision Makers

Today, the strategic decision makers in the industry are almost always involved in the e-transformation process. However, their involvement is more often than not, accidental. This book will provide them with fairly robust approaches that transcend mere technological considerations, in attempting and managing e-transformations. This book will provide valuable information to decision makers in the industry to play *proactive* role in globalization processes. Furthermore, discussions on change management, project tracking, user training, etc., will be of immense interest to these audiences from the industry.

Students and Academics

Serious higher degree students, masters (Honors), Ph.D., as well as academic researchers and teachers will find the "research base" of this book and the accompanying teaching structure quite attractive. Each chapter is based on intensive research conducted by the authors, as well as significant literature review based on number of books, articles and Web sites. Each chapter starts with key points, leads into the discussion, is followed by a summary, and has detailed references, all providing invaluable help to the researcher. The topics within the book are organized in a way that facilitates classroom discussions and project work. Thus, for academic work, the material in this book can be used (and has been used by the authors) as for a full unit (subject) as a prescribed textbook. Units that have benefited by this material thus far include: global information systems, advance topics in e-business, IT project management, and business process reengineering, to name but a few.

Semantics

The authors firmly believe in gender-neutral language. *Person* is therefore used wherever possible. Use of *He* or *She* is used for convenience and readability and does not denote a particular gender. Quotes and other references have been left untouched.

		Mapping of the Chapters in this Book to a ONE Day Workshop		
Day	Session	Presentation & Discussion Workshop Topic	Relevant Chapters	Comments
1	8:30 – 10:00	Why Globalize?	I, II	Arguments for globalization and its effect on organizations are discussed.
	10:30 – 12:00	Approach to Globalization.	III, IV	The Global Enterprise Transition (GET) process is presented, together with its Enactment.
	1:30 – 3:00	Technologies for Globalization.	V	The underlying technologies that have made this possible.
	3:30 – 5:00	Case study (practical work)	VI	Applying GET to a hospital and helping it globalize.

We throughout the text refer not only to the authors, but also include the reader. Occasionally, *we* refer to the general ICT community of which the authors are members. Thus, a statement like "*we* need to follow a process" implies all in the ICT community need to follow a process.

Mapping to a Workshop

The material in this book has been presented as a one-day to half-day workshop at seminars and conferences. Here is a potential mapping of the book to the workshop that we hope the readers will find helpful, should they be required to conduct similar seminars.

Yi-chen Lan & Bhuvan Unhelkar
Sydney, Australia
July, 2004

Acknowledgments

Dinesh Arunatileka
Shiromi Arunatileka
Steve Cartland
Steve and Leigh Cunningham
Joanne Curry
Yogesh Deshpande
Vijay Khandelwal
Girish Mamdapur
Makis Marmaridis
Drs Mahendra & Kalyanee Nathadwarawala
Amit Pradhan
SD Pradhan
Mahesh Raisinghani
Prashant Risbud
Ketan Vanjara

We also wish to thank our respective families in their support during our effort.

Thanks to my loving and caring wife, Anna, and my children, Bruce and Emily. Also to my father, Wen-hsiung, and mother, Su-chen, for their moral support.

— Yi-chen Lan

Thanks to my wife, Asha, daughter, Sonki Priyadarshini, and son, Keshav Raja, as well as my extended family Girish & Chinar Mamdapur for all their moral support.

— Bhuvan Unhelkar

Chapter I

Global Enterprise Transitions

In this chapter we discuss:

- The background reasoning for global enterprise transitions (GET).
- The meaning of globalization.
- The four eras of global market evolution.
- The organizational transition scopes.
- The global enterprise transitions roadmap.

Globalization: Basic Reasoning

Globalization, especially in the business world of the 21st century, is inevitable. Today, almost all businesses face intense competition all around the globe. The rapid changes in the global environment force enterprises to seek suitable business strategies to sustain them. This leads enterprises to change the way they conduct and operate businesses, and transform themselves in a way that will enable them to cope with the global challenges, compete globally and eventually grow. The winners in this phenomenon are the companies that implement their business operations in the most creative and innovative manner possible. Needless to say, this is done through the incorporation of information and communication technology (ICT) into business strategies and goals. In the past few years, IT has been recognized as an imperative factor that drives companies towards global operations (Palvia et al., 2002).

Globalization is an all-pervasive phenomena in today's world, with the business providing a significant context to the overall process. As former U.S. President Bill Clinton (2002) stated in his address at the University of California, Berkeley:

> *"A world characterized not just by a global economy, but by a global information society. When I took the oath of office as President on January the 20th, 1993, there were only 50 sites on the World Wide Web. When I left office, there were over 350 million and rising. Today, they're probably somewhere around 500 million. There's never been anything like it."*

It has evidently indicated that the globalization process will not thrive without judicious exploitation of information technology. Consequently, the key words that emerge in performing innovative business operations are "globalization" and "information technology."

Consider how this globalization has evolved from the non-globalized business environment of the past. The report released by the Intergovernmental Panel on Climate Change — IPCC (2002) — described that "a per capita GDP growth rate of 2.5% per annum was achieved after World War II." This could be attributed primarily to the increasing closeness of the world community in terms of communication, interaction and dependency on each other. Subsequently, this closeness also drove many organizations to start expanding their business activities across borders with the aim of gaining more business opportunities and advantages. However, during that period in time, cross-border business activities were only limited to traditional trading of goods (for example, export and import of materials). The organizations undertaking this trade were still individually located in their home countries. Later, the world's day-to-day business operations were further transformed due to the invention of personal computers. The organizations' information flows (various presentations such as text, image, and voice) could be easily exchanged via an inconspicuous electronic cable (Blake, 1985). Finally the rapid evolution of computing technology to the Internet and the World Wide Web has brought organizations and countries together into a global village like never before. Consequently, the development of computers and the Internet have forced many organizations to reorganize their structure and business processes that would better enable them to handle the challenge of globalization, and capitalize on the opportunities. Thus, an acute need is felt to understand how the organizations can transition themselves to a global entity. This book undertakes the discussion on the reasons for and the process of Global Enterprise Transitions (GET).

In reviewing the literature for this book, the authors found little in the way of papers, articles or books that comprehensively discussed the overall management of issues in enterprise globalization. Although many researchers have addressed globalization issues, they appeared to be restricted to very specific areas. Culture, information technology and business strategy are some prevalent areas that appear as examples of "narrow" research. None of the literature provided organizations with a suitable abstract or high-level view of issues for the entire transition of an organization. Amalgamating the various global transition issues and constructing an abstract yet documented approach to the globalization process is the preliminary intention of this book. Additionally, there appears to be *lacunae* in discussing the relationship between the organizational structures and IT issues in the globalization process. Finally, there also appeared a lack of discussion on the probable impact of the organizational structure in global transformation. Without a clear understanding of these correlations between the organizational structure and the transformation vision, enterprises have no idea on how to even initialize the global transition process. Consequently, organizational structures, information technology, and socio-cultural impacts are issues that deserve detailed study in the context of global transition, as discussed in this book.

Understanding Globalization

Globalization is the conducting and the coordination of business structure, functions, activities, units, and employees together with the incorporation of appropriate strategies across geo-political borders. There are numerous factors required by enterprises to succeed in globalization. Firstly, enterprises need to recognize and employ an appropriate organizational structure. The organizational structure needs to reflect and facilitate the company's vision of globalization. Secondly, as information technology is the key enabler in global

Figure 1.1. Factors required by enterprises to succeed in globalization

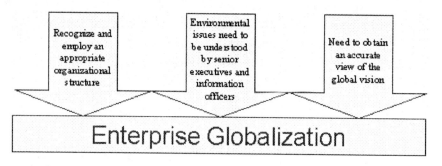

transition, its environmental issues need to be understood by senior executives and information officers. It is essential to do so prior to the application and incorporation of information technology in the globalization process. Thirdly, companies need to obtain an accurate view of the global vision to develop a transformation strategy. This can be done through the mapping of information and communication technology issues to the organizational structure. This is what is shown in Figure 1.1.

As is becoming evident, the global challenge has presented enterprises with new types of economic opportunities but at the same time significant threats. Accommodating these opportunities and threats by means of information technology, and developing a global IT transition framework to guide companies through the globalization process is crucial for successful globalization. This book underscores these important concerns faced by any enterprises moving toward becoming global organizations.

Global Market Evolution

Irrespective of the size of an enterprise and its specific industry, no business is isolated from the competitive pressures from elsewhere in the world. This is being felt by almost all industries and companies, and they must learn how to survive and prosper in the highly unstable and changeable global environment. The following briefly describes the evolution of global markets in four eras (Figure 1.2) (based on Moran & Riesenberger, 1996).

Figure 1.2. Global market evolution

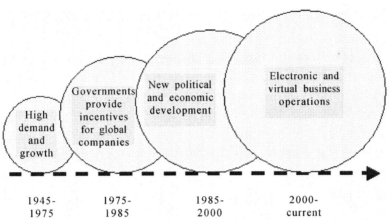

| 1945-
1975 | 1975-
1985 | 1985-
2000 | 2000-
current |

1945 – 1975

As mentioned at the start of this chapter, the 30 years following World War II marked an era characterized by high demand and growth. Economics of the free world flourished and the standard of living improved in most developed societies. Corporations focused on economies of scale and mass production to meet an insatiable market demand. Emphasis was placed on quantity and the efficient use of raw materials, labor and capital.

1975 – 1985

A fundamental shift occurred between the early-1970s and the mid-1980s. Increased production capabilities led to equilibrium and an eventual surplus supply in many industries. This fundamental shift changed corporate competitive advantages to those of increased quality, low cost and technological advances. Economies whose corporations were geared for premium quality, superior technology and low-cost production prospered. Governments began to provide incentives for global companies including lower tariffs, tax incentives and incentives to build new factories in their countries. Global economic growth began to slow.

1985 – 2000

The new political and economic development was unfolding rapidly. The emergence of regional trading blocs posed economic advantages for member states but will prove damaging for inter-bloc trade. The era of economic growth between 1945 and 1985 has been replaced by an era characterized by volatility and constant change. Those organizations that accept these changes as opportunities, and develop appropriate global strategic visions, organizational structures and core competencies to effectively capitalize on this new environment, will emerge as the victors. These political and economic developments are listed below.

- Governments are developing "regionalization" alliances such as the EU (the European Union), NAFTA (the North American Free Trade Association), and AFTA (the Asian Free Trade Association).
- Trends toward homogeneous technical standards will favor economies of scale.
- Increased telecommunications options at lower costs encourage globalization.
- Lowered costs and increased speed of delivery have stimulated global commerce.
- Global exposure to products through commerce, travel, advertising and TV has encouraged a more homogeneous demand for certain products.
- Competition from non-domestic competitors is increasing.
- There is increased exchange rate volatility due to global market demands.
- The increasing rate of technological change has encouraged firms to invest in R&D in multiple markets.

2000 – Current

This is the era of communication. The impact of Internet and Web services (WS) in this era brings about a noticeable paradigm shift in terms of what is meant by a global business, how the business relates to other businesses and how it manages its own internal processes that might themselves be geographically spread out. Most importantly, though, for this discussion is the manner in which an existing business transforms itself into a global business – in other words the process of e-transformation or globalization. The Web has enabled businesses to explore hitherto unknown frontiers, a view also corroborated by Deshpande et al. (2001) who correctly assert:

> *"With the advent of the World Wide Web, 'computing' has tran-scended the traditional computer science, information systems and software engineering in the sense that these three fields were strictly within the domain of a computing professional whereas the Web reaches the 'world'."*

Web services ascend even this "traditional" understanding of the Web, and make it imperative upon both technologists and business people to re-interpret the term "Web" and "globalization." This is so because Web services enable business organizations to transcend the "enterprise divide" that exists both between and inside organizations. In fact, Web services appear to hold the key to erasing international computing boundaries, and has left the door wide open to globalization and automation of tasks (Elliott and Unhelkar, 2003).

Globalization and E-Business Alliances

Why Should Organizations Globalize?

There are number of reasons why an organization would want to go global. When organizations form wider electronic alliances, it becomes imperative for them to also consider the issues related to physical alliances. This is especially true when the e-business alliance is global, spanning across geo-political borders wherein technological capabilities to interact with each other need to be supported by the physical capability to service clients and business partners. A global alliance effectively builds on the possibilities offered by two companies that are able to electronically communicate and have value to offer to each other. Usually, the underlying principle for electronic business alliances that also require physical alliance capabilities is that each member of the business alliance has something to offer that is complimentary to the other across geo-political borders. It usually turns out that one organization is a technically savvy global aspirant that is trying to reach across the borders. However, due to numerous factors such as social, cultural, legal and political, the organization is unable to transcend its borders. This is when the electronic commerce world facilitates formation of these alliances, as it is easier to communicate electronically across boundaries than it is to do so physically. However, the central point expounded in this chapter is that such alliances, although electronically (technologically) easily conceivable, require a corresponding understanding of the physical alliances for them to succeed. Therefore, whenever such alliances are formed, it is imperative that stakeholders and players in these partnering organizations quickly understand and establish working relationships that transgress the socio-cultural borders so evident in physical alliances. If employees and managers can effectively adopt different cultures, the companies will be benefited a lot by those cultures (Gupta, 2000). In fact, there are a number of benefits accorded to the electronic business alliances with a physical component in them that continue to promote the creation and sustenance of these alliances. We undertake a more detailed discussion of these reasons with an aim of creating a good background understanding of the causes of these alliances. Thereafter, we proceed to discuss the issues arising out of these alliances and the approach to mitigate them.

Who and Why Globalize?

The reasons why businesses attempt to globalize themselves have been discussed by number of authors in the past few years (Hartmann, 1997; McMullan, 1994). Based on numerous such discussions (e.g., Unhelkar, 2003a), the major reasons why businesses undertake global venture are identified as company maturity, current overseas trade, foreign market potential, exceptional overseas demand for the product, demand for a look-alike product abroad, knowledge capitalization, knowledge sharing, market expansion, customer service enhancement, risk apportionment, outsourcing, and legal and tax advantages.

In the subsequent paragraphs, we will expand on the above points in the context of the organizational structures and transition processes of the organizations going global.

Company Maturity

Getting into the global marketplace requires time, money and resources. If the enterprise does not have a good track record at home base and a history of stable performance, a global venture may strain its resources and complicate problems for its domestic operations and business activities (Hartmann, 1997). It is very important that the enterprise should be sure that it is meeting the demand for its products and services in the domestic market before branching out into the global arena. This maturity of organizations has been important even for virtual organizations in the dot-com era.

Current Overseas Trade

Orders from overseas customers suggest a potential market and point to a market niche that closer suppliers are not filling. The enterprise should consider visiting their overseas customers, and find out why they are buying their products. Visiting overseas customers may give the enterprise an opportunity to demonstrate its strengths to customers as well as acquiring a clear view of the overseas market. If the result of visiting shows that the overseas competitors have insufficient ability in their own domestic marketplace, it may indicate a positive suggestion for going global.

Foreign Market Potential

Conducting simple market research or reviewing competitors' financial statements would provide the enterprise an overview of the market other firms are servicing abroad. Collecting information about product origins from the overseas customers is another way of determining the market share of global competitors.

Exceptional Overseas Demand for the Product

Some products draw the whole world's attention. The enterprises producing these products probably cannot go wrong in their marketing plans. However, assessing which products fall into this category, would probably be the most difficult and risky thing for the enterprise.

Demand for a Look-Alike Product Abroad

A very important question the enterprise must ask itself is, "Do our products have the sort of appeal that will eventually tempt someone to copy them?" If the answer is positive, and the enterprise does not take these products to overseas, it will eventually be made by some foreign manufacturers and sell them in the market or even intrude the enterprise's domestic market. Although many developed and developing countries have adopted the copyright and intellectual property regulations, there is no guarantee to prevent imitation activity. For this reason, the enterprise needs to investigate the overseas markets in regard to its products' acceptance rate and the government's regulations.

Knowledge Capitalization

When two organizations from different regions come together, they invariably bring rich knowledge and know-how in terms of products and services offered. Collaborations between people belonging to these organizations, reinforced by information flow, make it possible for them to share knowledge, thereby enhancing the overall pool of expertise in the organization. This can lead to benefits such as faster innovation of new products, reduced duplication of efforts, savings in research and development costs, and enhanced employee satisfaction. Being able to share and build upon knowledge in order to create a richer set of knowledge is one of the major advantages of global alliances. Electronic technology facilitates these alliances, but the physical interaction between people is what eventually brings the knowledge to fruition.

Knowledge Sharing

In addition to creating new pools of knowledge, global e-business alliances also enable sharing of knowledge. On the social front, this is amply evident in fighting crime as well as the scourge of modern day terrorism. This is because in this age of communication, it is sharing of knowledge that takes even higher precedence than the existence and capitalization of such knowledge. In terms of e-business alliances, sharing of knowledge in the domains of processes, designs, engineering models, customer data, analytical techniques and so on, form substantial reasons for creation of such alliances.

Market Expansion

Market expansion has been considered as one of the basic reasons for formation of business alliances. Business alliances between two or more organizations enable the partnering organizations to have access to each other's customers, suppliers and the general markets where the organizations have been conducting business activities. It is understandable then that formation of a business alliance requires creation of a local know-how amongst all participating businesses. It is equally understandable that for some partnering businesses that are coming for a different "geo-political" climate, the social and cultural aspect of the local know-how may itself be too idiosyncratic to be relevant outside the particular local market. For example, a computer chip manufacturer in Japan wanting to sell its products through alliance partners in Australia would want to understand the cultural and social nuances of the Australia-New Zealand region before embarking on the market expansion journey. Another common example is of a bank in Hong Kong wanting to expand its markets in the USA. It will have to adopt to the socio-cultural value systems of the American market, which may be dramatically different than, say, the Gulf market, in terms of lending policies and value systems. Despite the challenges of differing cultures, however, businesses eventually find that through formation of alliances they are able to sell in a market that they had no access to earlier. Thus, while alliances enable businesses to sell in a foreign market, they also make it almost obligatory to understand and leverage the cultural nuances of those markets. Leveraging different cultures is not just a business advantage, it is also a business imperative (Teitler, 1999). Companies that develop best practices for managing culture capital find they are able to expand and supplement their e-business with physical growth. Without such best practices, however, they face the situation similar to the case study discussed by Unhelkar (2003b), wherein an Indian chemical manufacturing company rushes into its expansion in Australia and finds the going tough precisely due to lack of consideration to these socio-cultural factors.

Customer Service Enhancement

While a sale across borders may happen easily using electronic commerce, it is not always easy to service the same customer across boundaries. In many post-sale scenarios, as commonly experienced by customers buying cars and buying groceries, even local customer care is often uneven at best—let alone customer care across global markets. Global markets increase the risk of customer dissatisfaction or even customer churn. "Customer service is often seen as a necessary evil," says Raul Katz, a vice president with Booz-Allen and Hamilton. Good managers realize that in their business, customer service would be one vital element in holding onto premium customers in the face of competition. An example of enhanced customer service through alliances was that of IBM, which set up alliances with 61 software companies in 2001, up from its 50 alliances in year 2000. The expectation of IBM, through these global alliances, was that they will add up to $2 billion in new revenues in year 2001. Mike Gilpin, vice president and research leader of Giga Information Group says on these increasing partnerships that it "allows IBM to solve a wider percentage of their customers' problems." Bryce (2001) adds: "They can grow Global Services, do more outsourcing deals and provide more strategic assistance to clients." This is because IBM's alliance partners are available to provide service for products that may have been sold across boundaries in another country or region where IBM itself may not have had a physical presence. Thus, while e-business provides a single unified face to the customer because of global alliances, personalized and even peculiar needs of customers can be satisfied by the local know-how, expertise and physical presence of alliance partners. This not only results in a wider customer base but also higher volume growth from the same customers.

Risk Apportionment

Global e-business alliances are extremely helpful in spreading the risks to businesses arising, amongst other things, primarily due political instabilities. Global alliances provide excellent opportunities for strategic management of risks in businesses when they are operating out of unsure political climates. This, of course, requires that the issue of response to changing political circum- stances in different cultures is properly considered and integrated in the global response strategies of the business alliances that operate in global markets. In order that the management of a company keep track of all the changing technological, economic, political-legal, socio-cultural trends around the world, it is essential that they shift from a vertically organized, top-down type of organization to a more horizontally managed, interactive organization (Nuese et al., 1998). Horizontal structures are flexible, enable ordinary employees to play a crucial role by interacting amongst themselves, and enable spreading of risks due to vacillating external (in this context political) factors. Alliances with local players have a distinct advantage over traditional multinational company structures in this respect. For example, to gain access to China while ensuring a positive relationship with the often-restrictive Chinese government, Maytag Corporation formed a joint venture with the Chinese appliance maker, RSD (Adler, 2001).

Outsourcing

Although criticized in the current year (2004), politically charged climates of Australia and the USA, outsourcing plays a significant cause for business alliances, enabling alliance partners to capitalize on the unevenly distributed pools of skills and resources across the globe. By making it feasible for organizations to outsource certain routine work, typically to another country, there is potential for significant saving, as well as the ability to provide service round the clock (due to time differences around the world). This is invaluable, for example, in providing 24/7 call centers, which are themselves made possible through the electronic and communication medium. However, outsourcing usually comes with its own limitations in terms of social communication problems, understanding of what is meant within the contractual terms, understanding the requirements and agreement on what constitutes a quality deliverable. Furthermore, when strategic work is outsourced (as compared with routine work), it brings even greater challenges of the need to understand the direct and implied meanings behind all types of communications. These are the situations where excellence in business processes, use of industry standard modeling tools and techniques by partnering organizations and improving the overall communications between outsourcing partners, can play a crucial role in the success of such alliances.

Legal and Tax Advantages

Global alliances facilitate companies' ability to research, produce and sell legally, by taking advantages of the local rules and regulations of the governments of the environments where they operate. For example, stem cell research may be considered unacceptable, unethical or even illegal in some regions, but may well be acceptable in others. Alliances, especially at global level, are able to take advantages of the regulations spread across the globe, in order to achieve their goals. Alliances in the educational sector are common and popular examples of legal and tax advantages being used effectively in running a global business.

Organizational Transition Scope

Further to the aforementioned discussions, it is worth mentioning then when organizations are deciding their future business plans on pursuing a globalization strategy, they usually tend to focus on how the information systems can be transformed and aligned with the new global business strategy within the organizations. However, this one-dimensional assumption would prevent further expansion of business and information systems beyond the IT transition. On the other hand, the transition may try to include everything in one go, leading to chaos.

In accordance with Michael Porter's (1998) competitive forces model, to sustain a competitive edge in the global business environment, organizations must be aware of five basic competitive forces. The approach of aligning these forces to the organization's strategic plan determines the ultimate value of the global transition process. These forces are: the threat of new entrants, the threat of existing competitors, the threat of substitute products or services, the bargaining power of suppliers, and the bargaining power of customers. Each of these forces is delineated in the global business context in the following sections and the amended competitive forces model is illustrated in Figure 1.3. We also emphasize that the intra-organizational scope has the same level of importance as the inter-organizational scope.

- Threat of new entrants – these players are the potential competitors. They are not currently in the market. However, if the situation changes, they might decide to jump in. If so, they may be bigger, stronger, and gain more market share than other existing competitors.
- Threat of existing competitors – there are always competitors existing in any market. The current competitors can be seen as the key factor to force organizations in improving product quality, material costs, better customer services and so forth.
- Threat of substitute products or services – new technologies, new methodologies, and new approaches force the traditional products or

services into retirement mode. The replacements are better in quality, have effective costing, and are demanded by more customers. The threat compels organizations to keep updating their products and services through the incorporation of the latest technologies, methodologies, and approaches.

- Bargaining power of suppliers – the initial force comes from the availability of suppliers. If there are many suppliers available, the organization has the bargaining power to select the qualified suppliers. On the other hand, if there are only a few available, they will have businesses by the throat. Another force regards the relationships between suppliers and the organization. It mainly considers the relationship of sharing business vision and having common business goals. The closer their strategy and objectives, the tighter their relationships.

- Bargaining power of customers – similar to the bargaining power of suppliers. The force depends upon two main factors, the number of existing customers, and the relationships between customers and the organization.

Figure 1.3. Amended five competitive forces model (based on Porter, 1998)

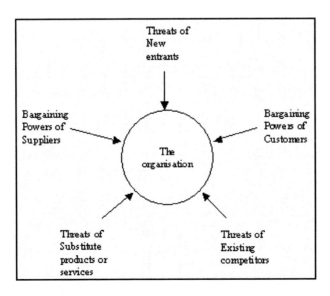

Further to understanding the current and future strategic visions, Andrew Grove (1999) and Bill Gates (1999) have also indicated the importance of organizational scopes (both inter- and intra-) as a part of the organizations strategic vision. In relation to Bill Gates' digital nervous system, it helps and facilitates an organization to manage its internal business operations as well as interact with the external parties such as customers, suppliers, and competitors. The digital nervous system supported by data warehouses, provides the strategic thinking for the organization as they exploit the data and elicit information and knowledge. A reflexive response refers to the organization responding rapidly to dynamic changes of external stimuli such as a sudden drop in market shares.

Based on Michael Porter's five competitive forces model, an additional force (the sixth force) — the force of complementors, was included to form Andres Grove's (1999) six competitive forces. The complementors are other businesses from whom customers purchase complementary products. Sometimes products or services only work with other products or services. For example, in the computer software and hardware situation, both support each other to demonstrate their functionalities. Consequently, the force of complementors can be seen as the mutual business strategy where organizations' products are aligned to maximize the business benefits.

When a business is in transition, the beginning and the end points are often identified while the transition in between remains as the unclear puzzle. Organizations should incorporate these competitive forces in order to derive an unambiguous roadmap towards the objective.

The organizational transition scope is further divided into two perspectives: intra-organizational scope and inter-organizational scope. The intra-organizational scope considers the core business competencies and their operations relating to the global transition. The inter-organizational scope outlines and discusses the importance of emerging new business processes, which are inter-

Table 1.1. Processes in intra- and inter-organizational scopes

Intra-organizational Scope	Inter-organizational Scope
Management and administration	Customer relationship management
Human resources	Supplier relationship management
Finance and accounts	
Purchase and procurement	
Sales and marketing	

connected among global business partners. Table 1.1 summarizes the processes involved in both intra- and inter-organizational scopes, which are further discussed in the following subsections.

Intra-Organizational Scope

When talking about intra-organizational operations, people are predominantly referring to internal business functions. Most of these business functions are generic to any and every enterprise, while some of them are quite unique and dependent upon industry types. From this research point of view, I would like to focus on the generic business functions that apply to global organizations as well as non-multinational corporations or small and medium-sized enterprises. These functions work together to lead the enterprise to survive and prosper. In general, five business functions exist in any of the above-mentioned organization types. These functions are management and administration, human resources, finance and accounts, purchase and procurement, and sales and marketing.

Management and Administration

The main tasks of the management and administration function comprise management of organization, corporate resources, corporate image, quality in all aspects, industrial relations, stakeholder relations, productivity, promotion of achievements, effective working relationships with external parties, liaising with political heads of sections or departments and administering services.

Human Resources

Human resources refers to management of all the employees. This function includes job analysis, position classification, employee training, employee selection, employee auditing and promotion, employee welfare, employee relations, work safety and sanitation, documentation and filing. The important tasks involved in human resources' function are development of a human resources plan and strategy, providing a workforce, management of industrial relations, employee compensation and benefits, internal communications, employees' amenities, and personnel statutory obligations.

Finance and Accounts

The finance and accounts function includes all the capital operations required by the entire enterprise activities. The major mission of financial activities is to deal with all the funds required by management, administration, sales, marketing, human resources, purchasing, procurement, and research and development, and to appropriately arrange the entire enterprise's financial resources.

Purchase and Procurement

The purchase and procurement function consists of all activities in relation to obtaining and managing materials, services or products required to be involved in the production processes from suppliers or vendors. The key tasks may include the management of stores, inventory controls, procurement management, receipts management, investigation and analysis of purchases and procurement sources, and shipping and clearing management.

Sales and Marketing

Sales and marketing refers to any transferring activities of products or services from producers to consumers. Sales activities are not only the traditional selling behaviors but also include the marketing mix or generally called "4P's" — production decision, pricing decision, promotion decision and place decision. Due to the rapid change in production techniques, many products have been supplied to the market efficiently. Many organizations have changed their operation philosophy from traditional production orientation to the modern marketing orientation. In other words, enterprises are now paying much attention to all the sales techniques and methods, focusing on the consumers' requirements, designing acceptable products for consumers and reducing product costs in order to arrange reasonable and competitive prices. Some key activities of sales and marketing can be identified as surveying the market, selling products, managing products and sales outlets, promoting products, and providing sales support and after sales services.

Inter-Organizational Scope

Inter-organizational transition scope focuses on the business activities and operations that are external to the organization. These external business activities and operations can be seen as the communication channels between the organization and other enterprises such as customers, suppliers, and competitors. By incorporating the external communication channels in the global transition strategy, a number of new business processes start emerging as part of the core business functions. As a result, these new processes extend the enterprise's organizational scope and change the organization's structure. Furthermore, inter-organizational technologies such as traditional EDI (Electronic Data Interchange), XML (Extensible Markup Language), VPN (Virtual Private Network), and Extranet are the key technological foundation to enable inter-organizational communications. These inter-organizational enabling technologies are discussed in more detail in Chapter V.

Following subsections discuss the new emerging business processes including customer relationship management (CRM), supplier relationship management (SRM), supply and chain management (SCM).

Customer Relationship Management

Swift (2001) defines CRM as "an enterprise approach to understanding and influencing customer behavior through meaningful communications in order to improve customer acquisition, customer retention, customer loyalty, and customer profitability." The fundamentals of CRM function in an organization can be designed to fulfill the global customer satisfaction through a number of categories. These categories comprise the CRM strategy, sales force automation, marketing automation, customer support center, e-enabled CRM, and the supporting technology and infrastructure for CRM implementation.

- CRM strategy — should align with or be part of the global business strategy. It refers to the plan for developing comprehensive customer related functions by integrating people, process and technology to maximize relationships with all customers. The basic principles of CRM strategy may involve aligning the organization around customers, sharing information across the entire business, leveraging data from disparate sources to better understand the customers and anticipate their needs, and maximizing customer profitability.

- Sales automation – involves the use of a multi-channel selling system that might include the direct/automatic delivery of products or services to the customers. The objective is to make the customer the focus of sales efforts by integrating customer needs into service channels and product strategies through the use of network sensors, microprocessor intelligence, and wireless communication.

- Marketing automation – refers to the utilization of technologies to an organization's marketing process. The modern marketing strategy involves the combination of traditional off-line and online media channels, and taking advantage of the Internet and technology to drive the B2C (business-to-customer) and B2B (business-to-business) processes. The marketing initiatives involved in the organization's CRM function including personalization, profiling and segmentation, telemarketing, e-mail marketing, and campaign management. These projects are designed to fulfill customers' requirements by providing the right products and services at the right time.

- Customer support center – refers to a single multi-channel gateway that integrates all customer contact points and provides necessary services. No matter what the presentation of the customer support center, whether it is a help desk, a call center, or an online support via e-mail or chat, the key concept is to provide the services and support to customers at any possible point and to present the customer with a positive impression and experience of the organization.

- E-enabled CRM – refers to the customer management tasks for business activities and operations through the Internet. The e-commerce capabilities such as online shopping, marketplace (online auction sites), process of online transaction and payment, and e-commerce security need to be addressed. These capabilities can be essential to successful e-CRM depending upon the organization's readiness of handling Internet trading and transactions through various methods.

- Supporting technology and infrastructure from CRM – in order to implement a thriving CRM system, the organization needs to apply the flexible information architecture and applications that will cope with the implementation of new business tasks as well as the resolution of technological issues. The new business tasks may include migration management, change management, and comprehending organizational culture and behavior change. The technological resolutions comprise the utilization of knowledge-based systems, data warehousing and mining, introduction of software applications outsourcing concepts or Application Service Providers (ASPs), the fundamental information systems connectivity, integration with back-end systems, and maintenance and upgrading plans.

Supplier Relationship Management

Supplier chain management has become the most influential practice in improving business operations and increasing commercial profits today (Poirier, 1999). The components of supply chain management embrace a large portion of entire enterprise operations and involve numerous business processes such as procurement, logistics, production, transportation, warehousing, delivery, and distribution. In order to construct and maintain an effective supply chain management system, these business processes are required to connect together with the integration of suppliers, retailers, distributors, and consumers to form a supply chain network (Figure 1.4).

In the global business environment, the supply chain network strategy is often the essential factor to reduce costs in material purchases, storage and logistics requirements, and product transportation and distribution processes. In other words, a successful global supply chain strategy requires the collaboration of

Figure 1.4. Supply chain network

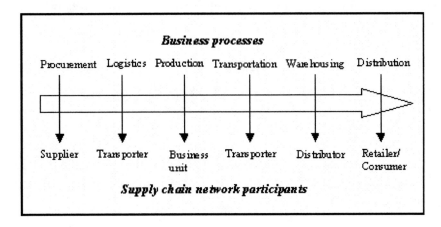

Figure 1.5. Internet information-sharing model for global supply chain network

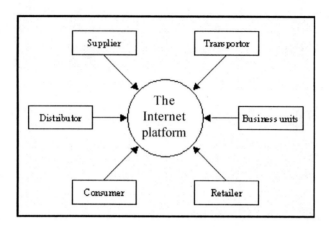

global suppliers, transporters, distributors, consumers, and business units. To achieve this goal, enterprises need to introduce the concept of information sharing in the global supply chain network. Information sharing amongst all parties in the global supply chain network can be implemented through the traditional EDI technology, or through the contemporary Internet platform (Figure 1.5).

However, the major barrier to performing the information-sharing concept is the trust between the enterprise and other supply chain participants. It is believed that many enterprises treat their business information as top secret and would never share it with outsiders, including their trading partners. Thus, when developing the global supply chain management process, enterprises need to consider not only all contributors and business processes involved in the network, but realizing the problems may occur in establishing information sharing linkages amongst supply chain participants.

The "Get" Process

Having discussed the reasons and scope for globalization, we now delve into the discussion on how such an approach to globalization should be undertaken. Figure 1.6 illustrates the transition roadmap towards enterprise globalization. This involves:

Figure 1.6. Globalization transition roadmap

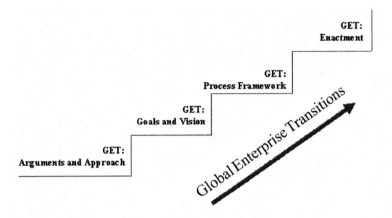

- Arguments for globalization.
- Goals and vision of a globalized organization.
- Having a process framework.
- Enacting the process of GET.

Arguments and Approach

This is the initial step of the global enterprise transition roadmap. It starts with delineating what is the global enterprise transition. Secondly, the global market evolution is presented to provide readers an overview of how the global market evolved. It is followed by identifying and exploring the reasons for enterprise pursuing globalization and defining the scope of organizational transition.

Goals and Vision

In order to succeed in global transformation, it is imperative to identify and understand the goals and visions of the enterprise globalization process. Furthermore, the environmental factors that influence globalization are thoroughly delineated to endorse the business globalization tendency. Then it is followed by an unambiguous description of the global strategic vision. Lastly, a comprehensive investigation of organization structures and characteristics are presented.

Process Framework

As per any business development or transformation, companies require a methodical framework for the transition process towards globalization. The process framework is developed to serve this purpose. The fundamental principle of the framework is based on the amalgamation of all studies presented in this book and the incorporation of a quality assurance scheme to ensure the excellence of construction. Organizations are suggested to go along with the framework for the successful globalization transition.

Enactment

Enactment of the global enterprise transitions process guides organizations from the theoretical perspective to the practical operation. It is imperative that all practical activities required in the global transition are understood and presented to the organizations. Although the process framework highlighted in the previous stage can provide organizations an overview of the global transitions, it is certainly not sufficient for organizations to apply it in the practical operation. In order to allow organizations executing the complex global transition tasks, activities involved in the enactment operations are partitioned into small components and presented in a systematic fashion. These systematic activities include launching the global transition, ensuring the GET process plan is followed, ensuring the executive consensus and support, managing resources, managing time and budgets, deploying business units or alliances in foreign markets, training and knowledge dissipation, managing organizational changes, identifying the review and feedback mechanisms, and verifying the efficacy of the transitions.

In addition to the above four phases, there is also an underpinning of ICT. The technology is separately discussed in Chapter V of this book.

Summary

This chapter provided the basis for why the organization should globalize in the first place. Arguments and scope for the process of global enterprise transition (GET) was provided in this chapter. Issues related to global e-business alliances, their significance and impact on globalization was also discussed in this chapter. Based on this discussion, we now move to Chapter II, wherein we discuss the vision and structure of the globalized enterprise.

References

Adler, I. (2001, July). Merger mess. *Business Mexico*.

Blake, R. K. (1985). Integrated networks: A realistic approach. *Telephone Engineer & Management, 89*(11), 64-69.

Bryce R. (2001, August 29). IBM Partners Up. *Interactive Week*.

Clinton, B. (2002). Transcript of Bill Clinton at UC Berkeley 1/29/02. Retrieved July 20, 2002 from the World Wide Web at: *http://www.berkeley.edu/news/features/2002/clinton/clinton-transcript.html*

Deshpande, Y., Murugesan, S., & Hansen, S. (2001). Web engineering: Beyond CS, IS and SE evolutionary and non-engineering perspectives. In S. Murugesan & Y. Deshpande (Eds.), *Web engineering: Managing diversity and complexity of Web application development*. Springer.

Elliott, R., & Unhelkar, B. (2003). The role of Web services in e-business and globalization. *Proceedings of 4th International We-B Conference 2003, Perth, Western Australia, 24th – 25th Nov, 2003*. Retrieved from the World Wide Web at: *www.we-bcentre.com/web2003/*

Gates, B. (1999). *Business @ the speed of though: Using a digital nervous system* (p.14-15). England: Penguin Books,.

Grove A. (1999). *Only the paranoid survive: how to exploit the crisis points that challenge every company and career* (pp.27-30). Bantam Doubleday Dell.

Gupta, A. K. (2000, March). Managing global expansion: A conceptual framework. *Business Horizons.* Retrieved from the World Wide Web at: *www.zdnet.com*

Hartmann, E. J. (1997). Going international: How do you get there from here? *Franchising World, 29*(2), 30-34.

IPCC Secretariat. (2002). IPCC special report on emissions scenarios. C/O World Meteorological Organization. Retrieved February 23, 2002 from the World Wide Web at: *http://www.grida.no/climate/ipcc/emission/058.htm*

McMullan, W. E. (1994). Going global on startup: a case study. *Technovation, 14*(3), 141-143.

Moran, R. T., & Riesenberger, J. R. (1996). *The global challenge: building the new worldwide enterprise.* UK: McGraw-Hill.

Nuese, C J., Cornell, J.E., & Park, S.C. (1998). Facilitating high-tech international business alliances. *Engineering Management Journal, 10*(1), 25-33.

Palvia, P. C., Palvia, S. C, & Whitworth, J. E. (2002). Global information technology management environment: Representative world issues. In P.C. Palvia, S.C. Palvia, & E.M. Roche (Eds.), *Global information technology and electronic commerce: Issues for the new millennium* (p. 2). Georgia: Ivy League .

Porter, M. E. (1998). *On competition* (pp.166-167). MA: Harvard Business School .

Swift, R. S. (2001). *Accelerating customer relationships: Using CRM and relationship technologies* (p.12). NJ: Prentice Hall PTR.

Teitler, M. (1999). Alliances are not mergers: What problems should you expect? *Nonprofit World, 17*(2), 51-53.

Unhelkar, B. (2003a). Understanding the impact of cultural issues in global e-business alliances. *Proceedings of 4th International We-B Conference 2003, Perth, Western Australia, 24th – 25th Nov, 2003.* Retrieved from the World Wide Web at: *www.we-bcentre.com/web2003/*

Unhelkar, B. (2003b, Jan-Feb). New beginnings: Case study on setting up Indian chemical engineering business in Australia. *Management Today, magazine of the Australian Institute of Management.*

Chapter II

Global Enterprises - Visions and Structures

In this chapter we discuss:

- The global strategic vision.
- Key elements of strategic thinking.
- The global organizational structures and the relating enterprise characteristics.
- Developing a global enterprise vision.
- Global management and organizational structures.

Global Strategic Vision

What is "Strategic Vision"?

Successful globalization requires good strategic vision and its implementation. Strategic vision refers to what an enterprise expects to be its ideal image in the long-term future. In the context of globalization, this ideal image is a primary driver for the enterprise's planning and implementation of GET. The guideline for such an envisioning process will be the planning of a strategic vision for the enterprise's future position. In this regard, it is worth noting what Tregoe and Tobia (1990) have to say:

> *"In the companies we know that are successfully making the transition to a more collaborative organization, the key to success is developing and then living by a common strategic vision. When you agree on an overall direction, you can be flexible about the means to achieve it. …. Really powerful visions are simply told. The Ten Commandments, the Declaration of Independence, a Winston Churchill World War II speech — all present messages that are so simple and direct you can almost touch them. Our corporate strategies should be equally compelling."*

It is vital for the success of GET that we develop a strategic vision of a global organization that is as palpable as some of the visions in day-to-day lives.

Strategic Thinking

The strategic thinking process can be thought of as the procedure of strategic vision development. Senior managers are normally required to develop the best strategic vision for their enterprises. This requires them to carefully evaluate the enterprise and the trends of the entire future business environment in which the enterprise exists. Development of a long-term vision (such as in 10- or 20-year plans) can vary from industry to industry. For instance, the oil industry may have a 50-year strategic vision, however the fashion industry may have only a one-year plan, due to rapid changes in the business and its content.

Senior managers should consider how their enterprises will be in the global future, what sort of knowledge and skills they should have under control and what aspects should be developed. Production, services, markets and con-sumers within the global context also need be stated explicitly. In addition, they should carry out a detailed analysis of the competitors' current and future growth, and develop a desirable organizational structure in order to implement the strategic vision.

Based on Tregoe, Zimmerman, Smith and Tobia's organizational strategic framework and driving forces (Tregoe and Tobia, 1990), the procedures of strategic thinking process are expanded in the global context as follows.

Understanding of Current Strategic Vision

Firstly, the enterprise should understand its current strategic plan. Before developing an ideal strategic vision, everyone in the enterprise should agree on the need for such a strategic vision. Conditions of a current strategic vision will be:

- Listing all present successful products and services.
- Listing current major markets and customer service's domain.
- Identifying existing suppliers who have provided services and materials/ products for the business operations.
- Determining the organizational core values such as employees' expertise, knowledge, skills and goals/objectives.
- Outlining the management style and organizational structure of the enterprise.
- Identifying the regulations and conditions imposed by the governments.

Evaluating Critical Factors in Global Strategic Vision

Global Chief Executive Officers (CEOs) and senior managers should be careful in identifying and evaluating each individual factor and understanding these factors in both positive and negative influences. These critical factors are listed below.

- General characteristics of successful products or services, markets and consumer domains.
- The enterprise's core capability.
- The enterprise's weaknesses.
- Characteristics of future products or services, markets and consumer domains.
- Current and potential competitors.

Developing Preliminary Global Strategic Vision

After the critical factors have been determined, the enterprise's CEOs and the senior managers can start developing a preliminary global strategic vision. The purpose of this part is to find the driving forces that will influence organizational performance. Thereupon, the management team can determine the driving force that best represents the enterprise's advantage. A number of essential processes should be carried out in this step.

- Focus on future strategy and set up a reasonable time framework.
- Develop a future driving force.
- Create a market and territory for future products and services.
- Develop competitive advantage and its necessary capability.
- Develop the enterprise's growth, scope and investment return objectives.
- Develop the relationships among global customers.
- Construct the global human resources management systems to enrich the global employees' capabilities.
- Develop the global integrated supply chain systems to enhance the related business operations.
- Incorporate the government regulations and required conditions into the business policies.

Examining Preliminary Global Strategic Vision

During the strategic thinking process, the process variation and transformation obstacles should be determined by examining the preliminary global strategic vision. The examination should include the following items:

- Current strategy.
- Evaluation of conditions.
- Core values.
- The enterprise policy and the actual operations.
- Identification and investigation of major competitors.

Management level should compare the future possible global strategic vision with the current strategic vision, and some basic questions should include:

- What are the differences between both strategies?
- What sort of variations should the enterprises perform when they start new products, services, markets and consumer domains?
- Are there any differences in driving force? How are they going to affect the business operations?
- Are they having the same capability? How are they going to affect the business operations?

Settling New Global Strategic Vision and Mission Description

The outcome of the examination step is the number of critical factors that will become the significant key factors in assisting new global strategic vision development. When these factors are finalized, the development of new global strategic vision can commence.

The organizational mission description focuses on the enterprise's future idea, resource allocation, and the planning of long-term and actual business operations. The mission description is the epitome of the global strategic vision and it covers information of the enterprise's core values, driving force, future products and services areas, future markets and consumer domains, and competitive advantages.

A successful mission description should include the enterprise's objectives, products, markets and technology information, core values, business operation philosophy, public image and financial aim.

Discovering Critical Key Issues

Critical key issues can be discovered during the transition of the global strategic vision development. These issues usually cause enterprises to modify the current systems, resources, expertise, skills, or structural frameworks.

Plan Implementation

After passing through the previous phases, the newly developed global strategic vision is now ready to implement. The strategic vision is transient. It should be maintained and modified in accordance with varying situations in the global business environment, market requirements and technology evolution.

Key Elements of Strategic Thinking

There are always some driving forces in each enterprise that lead the company towards its next stage. The concept of a driving force is the component that gives the enterprise momentum and drives the enterprise toward its expected direction. Based on Robert Michel's (1998) important enterprise strategic areas, the key elements of driving forces are identified and classified into various categories (Figure 2.1, Table 2.1).

Although these ten strategic areas can be found in the enterprise, only one of them is strategically important to the enterprise and is the main imperative to drive the enterprise toward success. CEOs and senior managers should determine which area of driving force is the most appropriate one to represent the business nature of their enterprises, and develop their strategic planning process based on this specific driving force.

Figure 2.1. Enterprise strategic areas

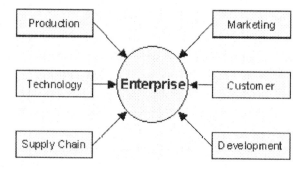

Table 2.1. Enterprise strategic areas

Strategic areas	Definitions
Production	Product/Service Concept – A product-driven company is one that has "tied" its business to a certain "product concept." As a result, this company's future products will greatly resemble its current and past products. Future products will be modifications, adaptations, or extensions of current products. Future products will be derivatives of existing products.
	Production Capacity/Capability – This company usually has a substantial investment in its production facility and the strategy is to "keep it running" or "keep it full." Therefore, such a company will pursue any product, customer, or market that can optimize whatever the production facility can handle.
Customer	User/Customer Class – The company pursuing this strategy has decided to "anchor" its business to a class of users. It then communicates continuously with that user or customer to identify a variety of needs. Products are then made to satisfy those needs. A user-driven company places its destiny in the hands of that customer or user.
Marketing	Market Type – This company is one that has "anchored" its business to a describable or circumscribable market type or category as opposed to a class of users.
	Sales/Marketing Method – This company has a unique way of getting an order from its customer. All products or services offered must make use of this selling technique. The company does not entertain products that cannot be sold through its sales method, nor will it solicit customers that cannot be reached through this selling or marketing method.
Technology	This organization uses technology to gain competitive advantage. It fosters the ability to develop or acquire hard technology or soft technology, and then looks for applications for that technology. When an application is found, the organization develops products and infuses into these products a portion of its technology, which brings differentiation to the product.
Supply Chain	Distribution Method – Companies that have a unique way of getting their product or service from their place to their customer's place are pursuing a distribution method-driven strategy.
	Natural Resource – When access to or pursuit of natural resources is the key to a company's survival, then that company is natural resource-driven.
Development	Size/Growth – Companies that are interested in growth for growth's sake or for economies of scale are usually pursuing a strategy of size/growth. All decisions are made to increase size or growth.
	Profit/Return – Whenever a company's only criterion for entering a marketplace or offering a product is profit, then that company is return/profit-driven.

Enterprise's Global Strategy

Development of global strategic thinking and global strategic vision is a challenge even for an organization that operates its business only domestically. The senior managers also confront a difficulty in developing a global strategy. During the process of globalization, senior managers should compare the global strategy development with the company's current strategy in terms of global environment factors, differences of global and domestic strategy, and the planning procedures provided by the subsidiaries and the entire enterprise.

Global Environment Factors

Consideration of global environment factors is a preliminary and an essential step when a domestic company intends to expand its business and market into the overseas environment. These global environment factors, discussed earlier in this chapter, are the following: global searching for sources, continuous development of new markets, scope of economy, trends in product-service consistency, lower costs in global transportation, government regulation, lower costs in telecommunications and equipment, trends in technology standards consistency, foreign competitors, increase of risks caused by exchange rate variation, the trend of expansion of customers from domestic to global markets, and rapid global technology transformation.

Differences of Global and Domestic Strategy

Not all products are suitable in the global strategy. Some products must remain domestic due to the government regulations, local tastes and significant costs in transportation. For example, food, drink and concrete manufacturers are represented in this category.

However, those products have the same characteristic, components or raw material requirements are the most likely to apply to global resource searching to find out how they can be operated in the global environment. The examples are computer and electronic manufacturing industries.

Global Integration of Planning Procedures

Developing a global strategy is more complex than developing a domestic strategy because global strategy development is required to travel across borders and integrate the various subsidiaries and headquarters senior managers' opinions. Senior managers are from various countries or regions, and their opinions and suggestions are critical in the process of global strategy development. Successful global strategy development must rely on the cooperation of each senior manager and the knowledge integration of subsidiaries and headquarters.

Investigation of a Global Organization

Enterprises that operate their businesses outside of their own countries need to decide upon and construct an appropriate organization structure in order to implement their global strategic visions. Each of the traditional organization structures has its advantages and drawbacks in the context of globalization. Global marketing demand forces the enterprise's leader to fully understand these organization structures, choose the most suitable structure for the enterprise's competitive advantage, and eliminate the limitations of the chosen structure.

Twelve environmental factors are considered obstacles in implementing functions of the traditional organization structure. The result of research conducted by Bartlett and Ghoshal (1987) determined that the key factors to a successful enterprise in the global market should achieve the following three elements concurrently, they are:

- Satisfaction of domestic market demand.
- Central control and coordination.
- Transference capability of knowledge and learning experience, and the subsequent creation of global enterprise.

Global integration development, domestic differences and the global creation of strategic advantages have become the enterprise's major challenge, and have forced the enterprise to develop its new organization structure in order to confront the global competition. When the enterprise's global strategic vision changes, the organization structure should be changed as well. The CEOs and senior managers should realize that the organization structure is the tool to lead the successful achievement of global strategic vision. The global strategic vision conducts the enterprise's future development direction, the enterprise's strategic plan is the method to lead us to achieve the strategic vision, and the organization structure will be the place that implements the strategic vision and plan.

Global Enterprise Characteristics

According to Bartlett and Ghoshal's (1998) three elements mentioned earlier, enterprises are suggested to review and improve their core organization characteristics in order to succeed in the global market. To further understand the global challenges faced by enterprises, Moran and Riesenberger (1996) have further expanded these three elements into a number of core organization characteristics. These core organization characteristics are outlined and discussed below.

Strategic Point of Emphasis

Each of the traditional organization structures has its obstacles in nature. It cannot achieve central control, coordination and satisfy domestic market demand at the same time. The CEOs are required to develop a strategic plan in accordance with the current situation and demand in order to achieve the expected central control, coordination and the standard of satisfying domestic market demand.

Global Strategic Vision

In order to develop a suitable global strategic vision for an enterprise, firstly, the CEOs should analyze the trend of environment factors, and review and inspect the enterprise and the industry's long term strategic plans. Discussion and revision should be brought to not only the CEO and the senior managers but also the overall employees in the enterprise. The developed global strategic vision should also be accepted and supported by all the employees in the enterprise.

Control and Coordination

A successful enterprise should develop a method that allows the enterprise itself to look after both the global coordination and central control, and this method includes:

- Productive scope economy.
- Development speed.
- Research and develop critical elements of centralization.
- Support more and more uniform products to satisfy more and more concurrent characteristic demand.
- Searching for global resources in raw materials and components.
- Eliminate or reduce the tariff obstacles.
- Standardize technology concurrently.
- Lower global transportation costs.
- Lower costs in telecommunication and equipment.

Domestic Autonomy

A successful enterprise allows its subsidiaries to make crucial decisions in accordance with the local market demand. The capability of rapid reaction to the local requirements will be the enterprise's key competitive advantage. Domestic autonomy should fully control the following points:

- Local taste and requirements.
- Local government protection strategy and trade obstacles.
- Threats by local competitors.
- Local regulations.
- Customized delivery specification.
- Difference in national standards.

Relationships between Headquarters, Subsidiaries and Local Markets

In an ideal situation, these organizations should have closed relationships, sharing information, and assisting each other. However, the multinational, international and global organization structures cannot satisfy these requirements. The management staff in headquarters and subsidiaries should be aware of the level of sharing information and communications between headquarters and subsidiary, between subsidiary to subsidiary and between subsidiary and the local market.

Enterprise Culture

Whether an enterprise will develop a uniform culture depends on the acceptance level of the global strategic vision by the employees overall. The development of enterprise culture is also influenced by the difference of the management level and the employee background, and culture experiences.

Selection of Senior Manager

The complexity of global business activity causes the enterprise to select an outstanding senior manager who possesses a different cultural background, has experiences in the domestic company and the headquarters, as well as the foreign subsidiaries. The CEO should reassign the potential senior manager candidates to the position that will have more interactions with customers and domestic or foreign subsidiary's personnel.

In order to implement effective coordination between subsidiaries, it is necessary to develop a corporate business language. For instance, if the enterprise uses English as a standard communication language, then the senior-level managers within the entire enterprise should be able to communicate in English. Thus, communication skills and language capability are the essential requirement for a senior manager.

Strategic Decision Process

Before making a strategic decision, the senior manager should have complete knowledge, information and clearly understand the enterprise's global strategic vision.

Information Flow

The management levels from the headquarters and subsidiaries should be aware of the information flow and knowledge control between organizations.

A successful enterprise may implement an information integration plan that will integrate the entire enterprise's information and knowledge flow, and will be maintained and managed by the enterprise's information systems.

Developing a Global Enterprise Vision

Having described thus far what the features and characteristics of a global organization are, and the fact that the enterprise strategic thinking key elements discussed earlier in this chapter provides the sound basis for such transition, we now outline what exactly are the relationships of the global organization with its customers, suppliers, management, employees and government. The discussion of these relationships clearly outlines the new global organization (Figure 2.2) – the way it should be!

Global Customer

Undoubtedly customers are the most important entity of most organizations. It is imperative for enterprises to understand and recognize their existing custom-

Figure 2.2. The global organization

ers in terms of the characteristics, requirements, and level of satisfaction.

First of all, each customer should be categorized in accordance with the level of importance. The important factors can be identified through the analysis of sales orders, the monthly sales total and the payment history. Customers determined as crucial ones are those who feature in a high monthly sales total with a correspondingly large volume of sales orders and acceptable payment schedules (no delays). Secondly, customer service programs should be developed to fulfill the requirements and achieve the level of satisfaction, particularly for those identified as crucial customers. The construction of appropriate customer service programs should consider several factors including the location of customers, customers' access times, creating a value-added supply chain, and developing or enhancing appropriate business processes to facilitate customers. Each of these factors is briefly delineated as follows:

- Location of customers – Customers are located everywhere in the world. When investigating the location of customers, organizations mainly concentrate on the analysis of product distribution. However, there are other concerns that also need to be addressed in relation to the location, which contains cultural diversity, taxation and regulation systems, distribution channels, and methods of transportation.

- Customers' access times – Further to the location of customers, organizations also need to recognize the time of access of information by each customer. In the global business environment, customers place orders and request services at anytime as necessary. It is imperative for organizations to ensure the information requested by customers is made available as needed.

- Creating a value-added supply chain – In order to provide customers with additional benefits over the purchased products, the improvement and effective management of the company's supply chain can be seen as an appropriate approach. To achieve this, firstly, the organization has to clearly identify each and all components of the supply chain and indicate the relationships between them. Once the processes and flows of the supply chain are determined, the analysis and redesign of the supply chain takes place to identify the improvement and develop value-added components.

- Developing or enhancing appropriate business processes – Activities and operations in association with customers are accommodated by several of the company's business processes. These business processes generally include ordering, production scheduling, delivering, accounting, and after-servicing. The functionality and concepts of these processes should be built to maximize customer benefits and facilitate customers in any circumstances.

Global Supplier

Managing suppliers is as important as managing customers. In today's competitive marketplace, many companies depend on suppliers to deliver materials, goods, or services that can be transformed into valuable products to provide to customers. Supplier relationships have become increasingly important to assure that companies remain on the competitive edge. Supplier relationship management can be seen as a subset of supply chain management, which pertains to understanding the important suppliers and maintaining strategic relationships. The Gartner Research group defines supplier relationship management as "the practices needed to establish the business rules, and the understanding needed for interacting with suppliers of products and services of varied criticality to the profitability of the enterprise" (2001). Furthermore, it is even more critical for global organizations to manage suppliers all over the world. Thus, effective global supplier relationship management is part of global information systems. It provides supplier intelligence through the integration of the internal enterprise's information systems and data obtained from the external suppliers.

Global Employee

The global employee of a global organization undertakes a unique combination of virtual and physical work as she proceeds with transitioning to globalization. As the organization becomes global, the work of the employee moves towards being more knowledge-based, as opposed to task-based, and the processes that are used by the employees traverse different departments and even different organizations that are coming together under a global organization umbrella. It is interesting to note that the effect of globalization also redefines the set views of a job. For example, in global organizations, employees will be connected to each other and to the customers almost all the time (or certainly the time and place of their choosing), resulting in the vanishing concept of a 9 a.m. to 5 p.m. job day. Finally, because of globalization, the concept of a well-defined career is also vanishing. For example, in the earlier days, a person could start a career in bank as a teller, move up to branch manager and then head a department. In a globalized bank, though, the well organized concept of a department, or even a branch, is diminishing. Therefore, the growth of individuals in global organizations will be lateral, as opposed to vertical (Unhelkar, 2002).

Global Governance

Electronic Governance is a crucial and integral part of the globalization process. This is because a globalized organization is bound to go across its geo-political domain, and come across customers, business partners and employees belonging to a different culture, society and working under a different government. This requires the globalized organization to create and maintain electronic and physical links with the government bodies in that region. Some of the core characteristics of relationships of a global organization with governments include the ability to understand and comply with legal and taxation issues, conform to the requirements of health, security and welfare of the employees, and distribution of funds.

Global Management and Organizational Structure

Management of a globalized organization is influenced by the organizational structures. There are four types of globalized organizational structures defined by Bartlett and Ghoshal (1998). The structures described by Bartlett and Ghoshal are: multinational, international, global, and transnational organizational structures. The following sections describe each of these organization structures in the context of the enterprise's core characteristics and the advantages/disadvantages of each structure respectively.

Multinational Organization Structure

The structure of a multinational organization (Figure 2.3) consists of the headquarters, as the top level of corporate management in the country of the enterprise's origin and a number of national and foreign independent subsidiaries. These subsidiaries are always required to report to the top level of corporate management. This centralized organization structure came originally from European countries. In the early stage of a traditional multinational organization, the appointed subsidiaries' general managers were always the senior managers at the top level of corporate management. The subsidiary's general manager usually had some kind of informal relationship with the CEO, and always reported to him/her directly. As the top level of corporate management has less knowledge of the local market, the subsidiary's general manager would be an extremely powerful autonomous authority over the subsidiaries. For this reason, headquarters and subsidiaries have an almost absolute difference in strategic vision, culture, business procedures and leadership. However, the subsidiary can directly communicate to the CEO and it is not required to have a lot of support from headquarters. With the independent operations and controls, the subsidiary has flexibility to support the local market demand.

Figure 2.3. Multinational organization structure

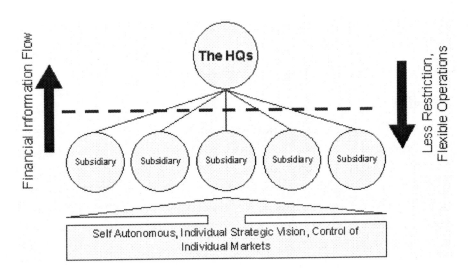

Table 2.2. Advantages and disadvantages of the multinational organization structure

Advantages	Disadvantages
Lower transportation costs. Easier to acquire the raw materials. Lower tax. Better control of local market demand. Reduced time spent on the product design adjustment. Subsidiary's general manager can communicate to the CEO directly. Reports are usually informal. Extremely high power in self-controlling. Less support required from the headquarters.	Lack of communication between subsidiaries. Lack of uniform strategic vision through the entire enterprise. Subsidiaries contest with each other for resources. Lack of information sharing between subsidiaries. Less cooperation and information exchange between the headquarters and the subsidiaries.

Three characteristics are defined in the multinational organization structure. They are:

- Management of assets and responsibilities are in the format of a decentralized federation.

- A simple financial information flow is used as a management method in between headquarters and subsidiaries.

- The global strategic vision defines the enterprise's worldwide operations as a portfolio of national businesses.

Table 2.2 shows the advantages and disadvantages of the multinational organization structure.

Enterprise's Core Characteristics

Strategic Point of Emphasis

The major strategy in a multinational enterprise is how to get benefits from the implementation of foreign autonomic subsidiaries. The advantage of this structure is that each foreign subsidiary can quickly respond to and can satisfy the local market demand, and they can be very flexible in order to control their consumers. The enterprise that adopts this structure will get bigger due to more foreign subsidiaries being set up. However, the enterprise will almost lose control of these subsidiaries' business activities.

Global Strategic Vision

Although the global strategic vision is developed by the headquarters, the actual implementation is always different from subsidiary to subsidiary. This is because of the lack of control coordination and control and over-independence of the subsidiaries, especially if the globalization is resulting from acquisitions.

Control and Coordination

In the three types of organization structures, the multinational organization structure is the lowest level of central coordination and control and has the least communication between subsidiaries. Subsidiaries always compete with each other for the limited resources from the headquarters.

Domestic Autonomy

The multinational organization structure has the most power in domestic autonomy. The subsidiary's general manager has supreme authority to decide and alter products to the market in accordance with experience of market demand.

Relationship between Headquarters and Subsidiaries

There are simple and informal communications between the CEO and the subsidiary's general managers. Due to the high autonomy, almost no information and knowledge flow is involved in the subsidiaries.

Relationship between Subsidiaries

Under the traditional multinational organization structure, each subsidiary faces its own business problems, language and culture differences. In addition, they compete with each other for limited resources from the headquarters and there is nearly no communication and information sharing activities between subsidiaries.

Enterprise Culture

Due to the highly autonomous nature of subsidiaries and the lack of interaction in information, knowledge and employees, each subsidiary has developed its own specific culture.

Selection of Senior Manager

In the development stage of multinational organizations, the subsidiaries' general managers are appointed by the headquarters. These general managers directly report to the CEO without any formal structure.

The headquarters' employees are employed from the location where the headquarters is situated and the subsidiary's employees are employed from where the subsidiary is situated.

Strategic Decision Process

There is a quite centralized strategic decision process. The headquarters has given the subsidiary quite flexible and autonomous operation authority.

Information Flow

There is almost no information and knowledge interaction between subsidiaries.

International Organization Structure

An enterprise with the international organization structure (Figure 2.4) contains a large national headquarters and a corresponding international department. These two departments report to the CEO directly. This kind of organization structure increases the control of non-national companies and provides frequent knowledge sharing and communications between subsidiaries. The main function of this structure is to transfer knowledge and expertise to foreign markets, which are less advanced in the development of technology and business operations. On the other hand, the local subsidiaries are free to adopt the new product, technology and strategy. This structural dependency concept is normally called a coordinated federation. An international organization structure originated around the time after World War II, when the American companies expanded their business operations to overseas markets.

The set-up of international departments provides a way of integrating foreign subsidiaries' requirements and submitting these requirements to headquarters. The advance of the enterprise headquarters depends on foreign business operations increasing the coordination between the foreign subsidiaries and the control of the foreign subsidiaries. It also provides a better implementation of the enterprise's global strategic vision. This organization structure gives great autonomous power to the subsidiary and the general manager of the subsidiary

Figure 2.4. International organization structure

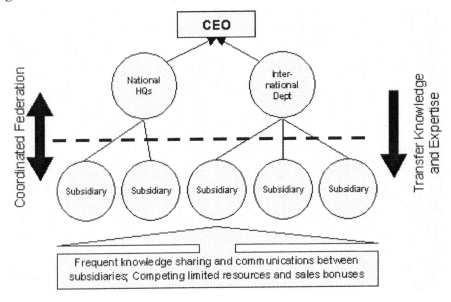

still retains a medium level of autonomy and flexible decision-making authority. However, the development and growth of the international department could cause conflict with the domestic headquarters, because these two departments will start competing for the enterprise's limited financial and human resources.

When an enterprise's organization structure has transformed from multinational to international, the role of the general manager changes accordingly. The subsidiary's general manager does not follow the informal communication path (report to the CEO directly) anymore. The general manger now must report to the head of the international department in a formal presentation. This will cause some of the general manager's autonomous authority to be stripped by the head of the international department.

In the initial stage of the international department development, most of the employees are from the domestic headquarters. Lack of knowledge in foreign markets, culture differences and international business operations cause difficulty for the implementation at this stage. Therefore, many enterprises still maintain their main research and development activities in the domestic headquarters and product development is still focused on the domestic market demand. The international market demand is only considered when the domestic market demand has been satisfied. Another disadvantage of the traditional international organization structure is that the design of the structure obstructs the employees' communication between headquarters and subsidiaries because most of the information and decisions are delivered through the employees from the international department.

The structured way that subsidiaries report to the head of the international department does not solve the communication problem between subsidiaries. However, subsidiaries still compete with each other in order to obtain the limited resources and sales achievement bonuses.

There are a number of advantages and disadvantages to an enterprise adopting the international organization structure. The following table (Table 2.3) identifies these advantages and disadvantages.

Enterprise's Core Characteristics

Strategic Point of Emphasis

The set-up of international departments can integrate the foreign business functions. The change of the global strategic vision is the major cause of structure transformation. The foreign subsidiary's general manager and em-

Table 2.3. Advantages and disadvantages of the international organization structure

Advantages	Disadvantages
The enterprise headquarters attaches much importance to the strategy of foreign business operations.	Causes potential competition in between the domestic headquarters and the international department.
International business integration has a crucial influence on the entire enterprise's organization structure.	Culture differences cause conflict between the domestic headquarters and the international department.
Increasing central control and coordination while the foreign subsidiaries still have quite flexible autonomous power.	Lack of training in across-border coordination due to the various countries of origin of subsidiaries' employees.
Provides a better development environment for managers of international departments.	Prevents a meeting of the minds between the domestic and international managers.
International departments can focus on developing new subsidiaries and support subsidiaries with uniform assistance.	Two different leadership styles and enterprise culture with semi-autonomous organizations (domestic headquarters and international department).
International departments have better control of manufacturing, raw materials and capital information in various places in order to make a better strategic decision.	Research and development tasks still remain domestically-oriented.

ployees have less autonomy and they are required to follow the orders announced by the international department. Some centralized business functions such as marketing, finance, trading and education advance the competitive advantage, and will assist the development of the enterprise.

Global Strategic Vision

The traditional international organization structure usually develops two sets of global strategic vision in order to satisfy different departments and market demand.

Control and Coordination

The central control and coordination of the traditional international organization structure is normally at the average level. The communication frequency of the knowledge, control and coordination between the domestic headquarters and the international department is still very low and sometimes conflict between two organizations may occur.

Domestic Autonomy

The foreign subsidiaries still retain their domestic autonomy, but the importance of strategic competitive advantage is far less than in the multinational organization structure. The enterprise's management level attaches much importance to control and coordination in the international department.

Relationship between the International Department and Subsidiaries

The communication between the domestic headquarters and the subsidiary must be formally relayed through the international department. This intermediate step may delay some crucial strategic decisions.

Relationship between Subsidiaries

Through the common market and planned training and some standardized operating principles provided by the international department, subsidiaries have a higher level of communication and coordination than the multinational organization structure.

Enterprise Culture

The enterprise usually has two different kinds of business culture, the domestic culture and the various countries' culture. The cause of two different cultures developing in the enterprise is due to the different background and method of business operations between the domestic headquarters and the international department.

Selection of Senior Manager

When the enterprise obtains the international organization structure, the role and responsibility of the general manager of the subsidiary changes accordingly. The general manager of the subsidiary should be able to effectively communicate with the senior management level in the international department. When the enterprise has reached the mature stage, the general manager and employees of the subsidiary are normally employed from the country or region where the subsidiary is located.

Strategic Decision Process

Subsidiaries under the international organization structure have less autonomous authority than the multinational organization structure. For this reason, the international department of the enterprise implements most of the strategic decisions.

Information Flow

Due to the nature of the international organization structure, organizations' emphases are on the central control and coordination, high communication frequency of knowledge and information between subsidiaries, the international department and headquarters.

Global Organization Structure

Global organization structure (Figure 2.5) refers to a highly centralized world headquarters enterprise. Most of the strategic decisions are made by the world headquarters and it usually does not request any suggestions from any national or international subsidiaries. The structural configuration is based on the central assets, resources and responsibilities and the business operations of foreign subsidiaries are limited to only sales and services. The configuration can be described as a centralized hub. All subsidiaries are treated equally no matter whether they are regional, national or international. In the global organization structure, the enterprise pursues maximum scope of economy efficiency and the fastest decision-making, and becomes a nationality-less corporation.

The global strategic vision in a global organization structure is developed and decided by the world headquarters. The consideration of the strategic vision decision is focused on the benefit of the entire enterprise. However, the individual subsidiary's benefit is expelled. In other words, all of the strategic decisions must be made based on the advantageousness of the entire business operation and implementation.

A global organization structure can be further classified into three types: global area structure, global product structure and global functional structure. There are many factors that should be considered before the enterprise decides to adopt one of these types. The factors are: maturity of the production line, level of coordination required across borders, scope economic importance, specific technologies required, level of product flexibility in satisfying various local market demands, and level of expected centralization.

Figure 2.5. Global organization structure

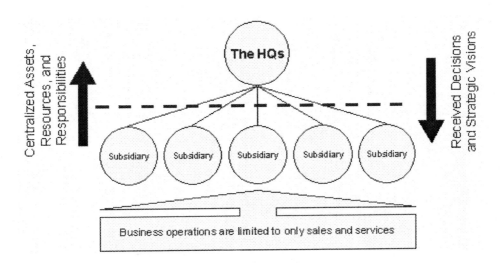

Global Area Structure

In a global area structure, all the subsidiaries within the region are treated equally. The enterprise's strategy is to ensure all regions focus on the same global strategic vision. The enterprise's domestic market has no special treatment for other regional markets. Each regional department tries to acquire resources and to manufacture products within its own region in order to get the best competitive advantage in its local markets. In general, the enterprise adopts the global area structure that has a narrow product scope within the mature market. The advantages and disadvantages of the global area structure are outlined in Table 2.4.

Global Product Structure

Global product department is created when the enterprise has transformed its organization structure from a domestic to a global product. This department has full responsibility for the global products in marketing activities, financial management and production. The senior manager in charge of the global product department has similar authority to the subsidiary's general manager. Each global product department is a profit center and has great flexibility in autonomous operation. An enterprise adopts this model when it is in an early development stage, and the main objective is to advance the level of global coordination. The enterprise that has better coordination can force the scope of economy, and increase the product knowledge and communication technol-

Table 2.4. Advantages and disadvantages of the global area structure

Advantages	Disadvantages
Regionalization provides better coordination between the scope of economy and domestic demand. The decision of regional strategy is made by the regional leader. Provides an integrated, centralized and focused global strategic vision. All regions are treated equally. Increases the communications between subsidiaries in the region.	Lack of communications between regions and the global headquarters. Regional-oriented mode has less focus of uniform product. Problems arise in the global product plan. Average level of centralization. Difficulty in research and development activities.

Table 2.5. Advantages and disadvantages of the global product structure

Advantages	Disadvantages
All the support functions are based on the product, not the region. Manufacturing of products is based on the customer's requirements. Research and development activity focuses on the global customer requirements. Emphasis on the global market and across border coordination. Provides an integrated, centralized and focused global strategic vision.	Duplicates support functions within each global product department. The senior manager of the global product department normally comes from the domestic marketing department. Subsidiary management focuses on pursuing the maximum investment returns.

ogy between countries. The global product structure provides an integrated and centralized global plan in order to advance each subsidiary's product promotion efficiency. It also offers the product's specification and characteristic adjustment to satisfy the various local market demands. Table 2.5 shows the advantages and disadvantages of the global product structure.

Global Functional Structure

Business functions are the major concern of enterprises adopting this model. In this model, each function is organized by the global headquarters. This is an unusual organization structure found in general business enterprises, but it can be found in natural resource industries such as mining and oil industries.

The advantages and disadvantages of the global functional structure are listed in Table 2.6.

Table 2.6. Advantages and disadvantages of the global functional structure

Advantages	Disadvantages
Small number of staff in the global headquarters. High level of centralization and coordination. Provides an integrated, centralized and focused global strategic vision. High level of functional expertise.	Difficult coordination in the regional production and marketing operation. Managers and staff have no responsibility in business achievements except for the CEO. Serious management problems due to the large number of production lines.

Enterprise's Core Characteristics

Strategic Point of Emphasis

In a global organization structure, the global headquarters organizes all business activities and pursues the global strategic vision as the only objective. The original domestic and international departments are dismissed and replaced by a global headquarters. All the regional markets are treated equally, and there will be no special treatment for the domestic market.

Global Strategic Vision

The global strategic vision is decided by the global headquarters and is consistent. In other words, the entire enterprise emphasizes the development and implementation of a single global strategic vision.

Control and Coordination

The strategy of the traditional global organization structure emphasizes centralization and coordination as the key to competitive advantage. The formation of this competitive advantage is the result of the creation of the global headquarters.

Domestic Autonomy

The enterprise does not emphasize the subsidiary's autonomous authority. Instead, it focuses on the scope of economy, global sourcing in raw materials, components, labor and capital.

Relationship between the Global Headquarters and Subsidiaries

The global headquarters and the subsidiary's management level have direct and frequent communication paths. As most decisions are made by the global headquarters, the strategy flow is top-down.

Relationship between Subsidiaries

Under the global organization structure, the regional leader is responsible for controlling and coordinating all subsidiaries within the region. However, subsidiaries within different regions have less communication with one another.

Enterprise Culture

The entire enterprise has a uniform strategic vision as its objective, and the enterprise culture is developed through the global headquarters.

Selection of Senior Manager

The enterprise's senior managers are selected from the general managers of the domestic or foreign subsidiaries even though they have less global business experience.

Strategic Decision Process

The strategic decision process in a global organization structure is highly centralized. The advantage of this is that each regional market has uniform products and faster market promotion.

Information Flow

Information flow is also highly centralized and the flow direction is normally from the global headquarters to subsidiaries.

Transnational Organization Structure

The development environment of the previous three (multinational, international, and global) organization structures was very different from today's market environment. None of them corresponds to the requirement of today's global integration, domestic differences and global creation. Each organization structure (multinational, international and global) has its strengths and weaknesses in facing today's economic environment. When the CEOs and senior managers choose one of these organization structures as their foundation, business operations and activities will encounter some obstacles or critical factors. Some critical questions include:

- Where will the industry go in the future?
- Where will the enterprise go in the future?

- How can the enterprise achieve its objective?

- Which organization structure can assist the enterprise in achieving the global strategic vision and plan?

- What are the advantages and drawbacks of the organization structure chosen?

- What issues will arise when the enterprise wishes to encompass the central control and coordination, satisfaction of domestic market demand, and transference capability of knowledge and learning experience?

In order to resolve the above critical questions, Bartlett and Ghoshal (1998) have devised the *"transnational solution."*

A transnational model contains a combination of the advantages of the traditional models (multinational, international and global).

> *"The transnational company defines the problem in very different terms. It seeks efficiency not for its own sake, but as a means to achieve global competitiveness. It acknowledges the importance of local responsiveness, but as a tool for achieving flexibility in international operations. Innovations are regarded as an outcome of a larger process of organizational learning that encompasses every member of the company. This redefinition of the issues allows managers of the transnational company to develop a broader perspective and leads to very different criteria for making choices."*

In the transnational model (Figure 2.6), the management of assets and re-sources are presented in both centralized and decentralized formats. Some of the assets and resources may need to be centralized in the enterprise's home country in order to realize the scope of economies, protect certain competen-cies and provide essential administration of enterprise management. Financial and business development functions are the typical resources that remain centralized in the enterprise's home country. In addition, some other assets may also be centralized in the transnational model, but it is not necessary to be in the enterprise's home country. For instance, a worldwide manufacturing plan of labor-intensive products may be located in the country that supplies a large number of workers with low salary rates. On the other hand, some resources

Figure 2.6. Transnational organization structure

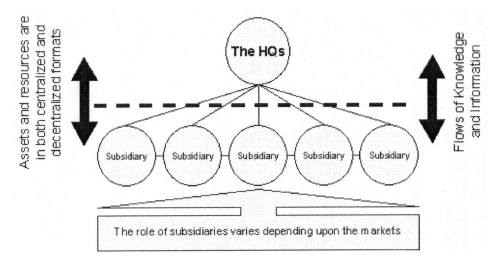

may be better decentralized on a local-to-local basis in order to create flexibility and to avoid exclusive dependence on a single facility. This may prevent some disruptions and unforeseen situations such as exchange rate fluctuation, strikes, and natural disasters. The selective decision of resources centralization and decentralization in the transnational organization structure is described as an integrated network.

Furthermore, the role of subsidiaries in the transnational structure varies in the business operations. In some markets, national subsidiaries adopt standard global products from headquarters and the role of the subsidiaries is limited to implementing the central decisions effectively. Some other subsidiaries are encouraged to differentiate or to develop products that other subsidiaries adopt. In this case, headquarters will give up its leadership power and hand it over to the subsidiary. In addition to the global products, there are a number of factors that are considered in determining the role of subsidiaries in the transnational model. These factors are government regulations, the availability of technologies and the position of global competitors.

Table 2.7. Comparison of four organization structures

Multinational	
Business operation mode	Decentralized Federation – each of the organization's foreign national units can modify the products and/or services to suit their national conditions.
Level of subsidiary dependency	Fully independent – subsidiaries have the authority and responsibility for their decision-marking and assets respectively.
Relationships between the HQs and subsidiaries	The HQs treats its foreign national units/subsidiaries as part of their international portfolio.
International	
Business operation mode	Coordinated Federation – knowledge and technology are transferred to the foreign subsidiaries that were less advanced in the market.
Level of subsidiary dependency	Partial dependency – the subsidiaries are dependant on the parent company for new products, services, processes, and ideas, although some responsibilities, resources, and decisions are decentralized.
Relationships between the HQs and subsidiaries	Foreign subsidiaries are considered as integral part of central domestic operation.
Global	
Business operation mode	Centralized Hub – allows the HQs to tightly control the foreign subsidiaries. Subsidiaries are limited to the sales and services of the standardized products provided by the HQs.
Level of subsidiary dependency	Fully dependency – the subsidiaries main role is to implement the policies and procedures developed by the HQs.
Relationships between the HQs and subsidiaries	The HQs treats the subsidiaries as a channel to a unified global market.
Transnational	
Business operation mode	Integrated Network – the subsidiaries are viewed as a valuable source of information, ideas, and skills, which can benefit the organization.
Level of subsidiary dependency	The organization is able to coordinate the foreign subsidiaries as well as giving these subsidiaries the ability to respond to their

Flows of knowledge and information are in both directions between headquarters and the subsidiary and from subsidiary to subsidiary in the transnational enterprise. Some knowledge or business solutions may be created by the joint effort of subsidiaries for the dispersed units. The competence of knowledge creation in subsidiaries balances the central solution dependency and provides the worldwide learning opportunity.

Based on the above discussion of the four organizational structures, the following table (Table 2.7) highlights the key characteristics of each structure to identify the boundaries between these different formations.

Summary

In this chapter, we discussed the visions and structures of a globalized organization. We discussed the effect of rapid changes in the global competitive market, which causes enterprises to transform their current business strategies and develop new strategic visions in order to advance their global competitive advantages. As a result of understanding and recognizing these global strategic visions and the enterprise's global characteristics, a global organization model is envisioned, which illustrates the components of the global organization. These components include customers, suppliers, management, employees and government. The need to understand and recognize the global strategic vision and the enterprise's global characteristics in GET was highlighted. Based on this information, we are now ready to consider, in Chapter 3, the process framework that will form the backbone of our transition plan.

References

Bartlett, C. A., & Ghoshal, S. (1987). Managing across borders: New strategic requirements (Part 1). *Sloan Management Review*, *28*(4), 7-17.

Bartlett, C. A., & Ghoshal, S. (1998). *Managing across borders: The transnational solution* (2nd ed.). MA: Harvard Business School Press.

Gartner Research. (2001, April). *Supplier relationship management: E-procurement's real value.*

Michel, R. (1988). *The strategist CEO* (pp.33-42). London: Quorum Books.

Moran R. T., & Riesenberger J. R. (1996). *The global challenge: Building the new worldwide enterprise.* UK: McGraw-Hill.

Poirier, C. C. (1999). *Advanced supply chain management: How to build a sustained competitive advantage* (p.1). CA: Berrett-Koehler Publishers.

Tregoe, B. B., & Tobia P. M. (1990). Strategy and the new American organization. *Industry Week, 239*(15).

Unhelkar, B. (2002, August/September). Vertical is not the only direction. *Information age, publication of the Australian computer society,* 20-23.

Chapter III

Systems and Processes Framework in Global Business Transition

In this chapter we discuss:

- The systems and processes framework for global enterprise transition.
- Global transition factors in business perspective.
- Global transition factors in human resources perspective.
- Global transition factors in end user perspective.
- Global transition factors in cultural perspective.
- Global transition factors in environmental perspective.
- Global transition factors in technology perspective.

Global Enterprise Transition Framework

Having argued for and created a vision of the global entity, we now consider the system and process framework for GET. During global transition, organizations often face many explicit as well as implicit factors that could delay or, in the worst cases, even destroy the globalization process. In order to eliminate these unnecessary incidents, enterprises need to identify, document and follow the activities of the process of GET.

In the past decade, researchers have made significant efforts to identify the global information systems management (GISM) activities. Most notable are Senn's six key information technology issues (Senn, 1992), and the eight multinational categories of global information technology challenges by Palvia and Saraswat (1992). Based on the implication of activities on the process of globalization, six categories are identified to facilitate classification and collation of the GISM activities (Figure 3.1). The core concept of categorization intends to provide the organizations with an abstract overview of concerns in relation to the transition to globalization. These categories are labeled as:

- Business
- Human Resources
- End User
- Cultural
- Environmental
- Technology

This chapter provides a detailed discussion of each activity and its underlying factors in relation to the global transition process.

Figure 3.1. Global transition factors

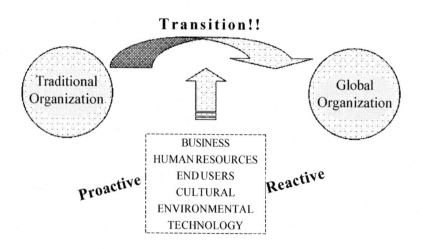

Business Factors in Globalization

In the process of globalization, business and information system strategies are often the senior executives' major concern. The alignment of global information strategies and the new business visions are crucial to the success of global business operations. Areas in this category and the transition implications contain: information systems planning, information systems organization alignment, information systems effectiveness, productivity measurement, business reengineering, competitive advantage, information quality, office automation, identification of global business opportunities, systems reliability, availability, and transferability. The following sub-sections investigate and explore these activities in detail.

Information Systems Planning

A global information system is a scheme that facilitates cross-border business operations by integrating both social and technical elements. Introducing a new global information system involves not only the hardware and software, but also changes in job specifications, skills requirements, management, and organization structure. All these changes should not be any surprise to all parties involved in the development and implementation of the new systems. In fact, the anticipated changes related to the new systems should be documented and the business plan should be drawn up to reflect all of the stages. Before the global transition process commences, the organization needs to develop an information system plan to state precisely the specifications and requirements of each phase and ensure that the plan matches the organization's strategic vision. As per Laudon and Laudon (2002), the information systems plan refers to:

> *"A roadmap indicating the direction of systems development: the rationale, the current situation, the management strategy, the implementation plan, and the budget."*

To develop an effective global information systems plan, the organization should first understand the current business status in terms of its strengths and weaknesses, recognize all activities faced in the global transition process, and clearly outline both short-term and long-term business strategies.

Information Systems Organization Alignment

It is imperative for the information system function to align itself with the business processes, strategies and goals of the organization. Information systems are developed based on the requirements, behaviors and activities of all business parties who have intercommunicated with the organization's core business functions and objectives. These parties include suppliers, customers, government agencies, and even competitors. The goals and strategic vision of these business entities must be incorporated in the development of information systems. In addition, the alignment of information systems with business functions in a global organization must also take into account the organizational type or structure. As mentioned in Chapter II, each of the four multinational organization types has quite distinct structures in terms of operational and managerial strategies. Information systems organization alignment in the global organization is not just following business processes and conducting analysis and design, it also requires understanding of the abstract level of business strategic vision and cooperation with all business entities.

Information Systems Effectiveness

Developing effective global information systems requires more than an understanding of business processes and applying the latest information technology. It requires the participation of people who will be using the information systems from all areas through the entire development life cycle. These users include senior managers, operational staff, salespeople, customers, suppliers, and many other general employees. All these users should be invited to participate in different development phases in accordance with their job-related processes or tasks. Thus, ascertaining the user involvement through the development phases is crucial for an effective global information system.

Productivity Measurement

An efficient and productive enterprise is built upon matured business processes. Accordingly, the measurement of productivity in the global organization should focus on benchmarking of business processes and information systems that facilitate these processes. The measurement of process maturity as set by the ISO (International Organization for Standardization), and the CMM

(Capability Maturity Model) can be used as software quality measurement. The ISO 9000:2000 standard is the latest version of the quality assurance system. It concerns quality systems that are assessed by outside auditors, and it applies to many kinds of production and manufacturing organizations. It covers documentation, design, development, production, testing, installation, servicing, and many other general business processes.

The CMM is developed by the SEI (Software Engineering Institute). It is a model of five levels of organizational maturity that determine effectiveness in delivering quality information system software.

Business Reengineering

As organizations pursue globalization, changes are foreseeable in four areas:

- Fundamental organization structure.
- Business processes.
- Management concepts.
- People and skills.

Of the above four, changes in business processes are tightly coupled with the design of global information systems. Organizations have to understand and recognize that business processes in the global context are significantly different from the traditional or existing ones. In order to design the appropriate information systems to facilitate business operations in the global environment, organizations should rethink and redesign the business processes to align with the global business strategic vision, in accordance with Hammer and Stanton's (1995) "official definition" of reengineering which is, "the fundamental rethinking and radical redesign of business processes to achieve dramatic improvements in performance."

Four key words (fundamental, radical, dramatic, and processes) contained in the definition are identified to further explore its significance in the globalization perspective.

- Fundamental – in preparing for business process reengineering, organizations must ask themselves questions in relation to the current and future business operations and strategic vision. These questions can be as simple as "what are the current business processes?", "what are the new business processes that would emerge after the global transition?", and "what are the activities involved in the processes (both current and future)?" and so forth. By asking these questions, organizations are forced to map an overall picture of ways they are expecting to conduct their global businesses.

- Radical – refers to the design of business process from its conception. Which means not just redesigning the business processes by making modifications or improvements to the existing ones. Instead, the key concept of reengineering is to remove the old ones and rebuild the new processes to cope with the global operations.

- Dramatic – refers to the deepness of changes to the existing business processes. Dramatic improvement differs from marginal improvement, as the former requires giving up the old ones and replacing them with something totally new, while the latter requires only fine-tuning of the existing processes.

- Processes – are the objects of the reengineering concept. A business process refers to a collection of activities that carry out operations to achieve business routines and satisfy customer requirements. In a global business environment, many business processes are accomplished through collaborative teams across borders. Hence, the view of trans-border business processes is crucial to success in the business reengineering process for global organizations.

In addition to Hammer and Champy's reengineering, Bill Gates (1999) has introduced the concept of a digital nervous system as the basis of the business communication network to facilitate the transformation or reengineering of business processes into new digital business processes.

Most of the business enterprises focus on a few essential elements such as customers, suppliers, products and services, costs, employees, and skills. Each of these areas contains a collection of business data. Through human intelligence, the data is interpreted and transformed into meaningful information to assist people at all levels to make decisions. However, if the interpretation and transformation are performed significantly by the use of information technology, then the organization has a digital nervous system. Gates describes a digital nervous system as,

" the digital processes that closely link every aspect of a company's thoughts and actions… The immediate availability of accurate information changes strategic thinking from a separate, stand-alone activity to an ongoing process integrated with regular business activities."

In thinking of business reengineering, Gates suggests organizations should consider three imperative concepts. At first organizations should review their current business processes periodically; second, they should try to have the least number of people involved in decision-making for each business process; and third, they should consolidate procedures and activities to decrease the failure rates.

Multinational corporations often find that some similar or even identical processes are implemented in various trans-border business units. This would result in the duplication of jobs, inappropriate allocation of human resources, and ambiguous global management responsibilities. Although creating a new business process or reengineering an existing one is a complex and sophisticated project in a global business organization, the process owners in all trans-border business units should define a unique global process that can be adopted throughout the organization. Furthermore, the globalized business processes streamline the transition in outsourcing situations.

Competitive Advantage

Attaining global competitive advantage, organizations require competence in changes in areas such as organizational structure, skills, and resources. These competences are crucial to attaining competitive advantage but perhaps even more important is making sure that the competitive advantage is always through value-adding for the customer. Ford Motor Company is a good example to illustrate how the changes have taken place (Leontiades, 2001). In order to reach global competitive advantage, Ford transformed its organizational structure through five stages of changes in its competence.

In the first stage, competence of overseas business units was based on products, designs and methods provided by the home country (the headquarters). In stage 2, competence of the overseas business unit was based on its own production with the designs and methods provided by the home country. When the overseas business unit had the capability of production and designing products locally, then it had reached the third stage. In the forth and fifth stages, the capability of production and design were based regionally and globally respectively. In accordance with the above stages, the competence of changes became the driver for the organization towards globalization, while customer requirements became the trigger of transformation from stage to stage. Furthermore, to maintain the global competitive edge, the organization needs to ensure the reorganization of the organizational structure and its business strategy have met with customer satisfaction in the global transformation process.

Besides the changes in competence, Porter (1998) also introduced the diamond theory of competitive advantage. The diamond constitutes four attributes that determine the environment, the inputs of production, the availability of resources, the requirement of necessary skills, the business strategy, and structure of the organization. These attributes are labeled as factor conditions, demand conditions, related and supporting industries, and firm strategy, structure and rivalry. Using the diamond of competitive advantage (Porter, 1998) in the globalization context (see Figure 3.2), the four determinants of the competitive advantage can be described as follows.

- Factor conditions – factors of production are the fundamental input to competition. The advantage arises from the high quality inputs such as

Figure 3.2. Modified diamond of competitive advantage in the global organization (based on Porter, 1998)

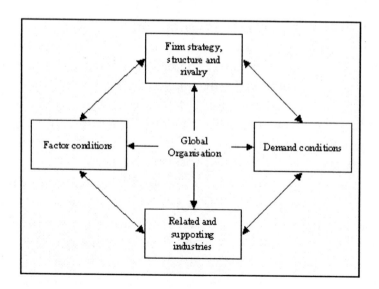

global market and product knowledge, diverse acquisition of technology and infrastructure and variety of human and capital resources.

- Demand conditions – advantages arise from the characteristic of global market and products. In a global market customers demand products from anywhere in the world. Redesigning products or services is essential to fulfill the global conditions and satisfy the global customer requirements. Thus, the global products can be manufactured anywhere and distributed to the nearest market.

- Related and supporting industries – advantages in increasing productivity arise from the availability of global resources (specialized suppliers and related industries). Through the global supplier channel, organizations are able to find required supporting materials and services at reduced costs. The presence of global resources also works better with the global production strategy. That is, the selected global suppliers provide the required materials or services directly to the closest global production sites. This results in the reduction of time required for transportation and thus shortens the production cycle.

- Firm strategy, structure, and rivalry – the diverse and multicultural conditions in the global business environment present advantages to enterprises in organizing, structuring, and managing the business strategy and structures to survive the global rivalry.

Information Quality

Information is a direct product of processes that capture knowledge about the persons, places, things and events discovered while conducting business transactions (English, 2001). In a global organization, the sources of information are enormous. Information is produced by virtually everyone from any level in the organization. As a result, enterprises often face situations such as missing or inaccurate information. This would cause business processes to fail and increase costs in reproducing information. Hence, organizations must apply quality principles to effectively manage information. However, managing and controlling information and its quality seem to be a complex and challenging task. Clikeman (1999) defines a number of dimensions that are critical to maintaining the information quality in the global organization. They are relevance, accuracy, timeliness, completeness, coherence, format, accessibility, compatibility, security, and validity.

Office Automation

Office automation involves the planned application of integrated information handling of tools and methods to improve the productivity of people in office operations. Although managing information by office people is the focus of office automation, other aspects of the office arc also affected. These include factors such as the structure of business functions and lines of reporting, training for new methods, work space design, locations of subsidiaries or business units, home versus office work, hours of work, employee morale, and job classifications. Organizations that harness office automation products will need to deal with much more than just technological activities.

Three major roles of an office identified by Laudon and Laudon (2002) are:

- Coordinate and manage the work of local professional and information workers within the organization.

- Link the work being performed across all levels and functions throughout the organization.

- Couple the organization with the external environment.

Generally, there are five major office activities that can be identified, including managing documents, scheduling individuals and groups, communicating with individuals and groups, managing data on individuals and groups, and managing projects. The computing and information technologies that support each activity should be identified and made available for all business units in planning for globalization.

- Managing Documents – it involves tasks such as creation, storage, retrieval, and dissemination. The technologies supporting these tasks include word processing, desktop publishing, document imaging, Web publishing, and work flow manager applications.

- Scheduling individuals and groups – the technologies that facilitate this activity include electronic calendars, groupware, and intranet.

- Communicating with individuals and groups – the tasks include initiating, receiving, and managing data in the format of voice, image, digital, and text. The supporting technologies may consist of e-mail, voice mail, digital answering systems, groupware, and intranets.

- Managing data on individuals and groups – this activity mainly focuses on the management of data and information of employees, customers, vendors, suppliers, or even competitors. The enabling technologies include database systems and spreadsheet applications.

- Managing projects – it refers to the management of collaborative work and projects in both local and global environments. The technologies that can be applied to this activity may include groupware, teamware, and project management applications.

Identification of Global Business Opportunities

- With rapidly advancing technology the business and information technology community is encouraged to consider many more innovative business models. These emerging innovative business models can be defined in a number of forms such as mergers and alliances, differentiation of products and services, e-business (electronic business), economic value-added focus, productivity process, order fulfillment and customer demand management, and globalization of markets.

- Mergers and alliances – this refers to the need for individual organizations to increase in size either by internal growth or alliances with external parties (other organizations).

- Differentiation of products and services – refers to the need to provide products and services to customers that are, at the same time, unique, value efficient, and reasonably priced.

- E-business – refers to development, acceptance, and usage of the Internet business tools in overall or partial company operations (such as virtual organization), sourcing and supply strategies.

- Economic value-added focus – refers to the increasing financial pressure on organizations to achieve high process performance as they affect or are affected by sourcing and supply, and increasing focus on economic value added.

- Productivity process – refers to the growing emphasis by top management on cost control, reduced cycle time, increasing flexibility, the profit picture and process economics.

- Order fulfillment and customer demand management – refers to the fundamental changes in distribution, and the need to change the methods used in customer order fulfillment and customer demand management.

- Globalization of markets – refers to the need to adopt standard processes for producing, selling and distributing products and services.

Systems Reliability, Availability, and Transferability

Information systems should be reliable in terms of withstanding use by various types of users through a variety of platforms or environments. This refers to the capability of incorporating diverse error handling strategies to react to any possible and unforeseeable situations in information systems. Moreover, the availability and transferability of information systems are considered as important as the systems reliability in the global organization. Due to the multinational business units in the global organization, each business unit may need to access the information in different time periods. The maintenance strategy needs to cope with this multinational characteristic to eliminate the consequences of the system's downtime. If the implementation of global information systems is through the Internet, users expect the systems to operate in a 24/7 manner. The components and modules of global information systems should also be designed flexibly enough to transfer and adapt from one business unit to another without further technical modifications. This portable and transferable concept should be built into the development architecture to enhance the reusability and to reduce the development and maintenance costs.

Human Resources Factors in Globalization

People are major players in designing, implementing and utilizing information systems. When investigating the human resources management in the global business environment, a number of areas need to be considered as crucial to the success of globalization. These areas are recruiting, training, organizational learning, cross-cultural skills development, and global team development (Lan, 2002).

Recruiting

Hiring employees for a global organization is not as easy as for domestic companies. The recruitment process requires careful planning to provide the best strategy for the global organization in obtaining suitable employees for appropriate positions and locations. For example, Unhelkar (2002) has suggested the importance of a "best fit" approach to recruitment. In preparation of the global recruitment plan, the organization's human resources department firstly needs to transform itself into a global operation. Traditionally, human resources is a quite independent and unique system for each subsidiary in multinational corporations (MNCs). For example, the human resources department in the Sydney subsidiary may have no relationships or connections with the human resources department in Tokyo of the same MNC. In addition, each subsidiary's human resources department may maintain its own operations that may be enough to fulfill the local requirements but certainly would not have the flexibility to facilitate the management of employees in the global scale. This uniqueness of the human resources function in the traditional organization leaves the organization with no centralized control and standardized operations in regard to people management. By implementing a global human resources system, MNCs would benefit in efficiently managing geographically dispersed employees as well as standardizing the organizations' employment policies.

In the global recruitment aspect, the Internet seems to be the appropriate operating platform. The implementation of a corporation's careers Web site is considered to be the key success factor in improving the speed, efficiency and effectiveness of the overall recruiting process. Further, the careers Web site has a profound impact on the organization's global recruitment strategy in the following areas (Jones, 2001):

- Branding and sourcing – it provides the potential candidates with a comprehensive and concentrated source of information and branding experience regarding the organization as an employer.
- Response management – it provides a standardized application for candidates from various sources and maintains a centralized database for the ongoing relationships.
- Assessment – to reduce the organization's costs and time, extra features can be incorporated into the careers Web site for pre-screening and filtering the candidates.

- Processing – it streamlines the processes of people/employee management by connecting the careers Web site to the organization's back-end systems.

Training

Training is a critical agenda for organizations to continuously improve the quality perspective in products, services and management aspects, and strengthens organizations searching for a global competitive edge. In designing and developing the training programs, a number of factors are identified to ensure appropriateness and effectiveness. These factors include:

- Stage in the global transition process – as there are various stages in the global transition process, the training development needs to reflect the various skills required by employees carrying out tasks at different stages.

- Target employee domains – different levels and types of employees would play different roles in the organization's global transition process. Considering the types of employees and their respective situations, the suitable training programs could be developed to enhance the employee skills and serve the requirements of globalization.

- Methods of training – implementing training programs across national borders has a significant level of complexity and budget requirements. By applying technology (such as computer-based training programs, or online training) to develop and deliver the training programs would allow the employees to participate in learning anywhere and anytime. However, the standardized training programs may require some variations, for example in languages and cultural aspects, to suit the foreign subsidiary contexts.

Organizational Learning

In today's challenging business marketplace, organizational learning seems to become one of the prominent aspects that enterprises would like to focus on and incorporate into their business strategies. As the enterprise evolves, many changes have transpired and are demanded for resolutions. These changes are often associated with leadership and management styles, implication of technology, and the business environment. As a result of swift technological development, enterprises are capable of applying knowledge management, and through the online learning environment to promote organizational learning. Laudon and Laudon (2002) define knowledge management as "the process of systematically and actively managing and leveraging the stores of knowledge in the organization." The key information systems that support knowledge management include office automation systems (OAS), knowledge work systems (KWS), group collaboration systems, and artificial intelligence systems (AI).

Cross-Cultural Skills Development

In multinational corporations, business units and subsidiaries are often spread across nations and have quite distinct cultural attitudes and characteristics. Hence, employees in global companies are more likely to have greater chances of dealing with foreign colleagues than non-multinational companies. In order to smooth out the communications and information flows between employees from different cultural backgrounds, global corporations should consider the introduction of multi-cultural skills development programs. These programs may consist of language and communication learning, and recognizing and understanding of culture differences.

Global Team Development and Leadership Styles

Teams take on a unique structure and format in a global environment. This is so because members of the team with different responsibilities may be physically sitting in different working environments and offices. Therefore, collaboration and coordination are the two imperative ingredients of successfully conducting teamwork in the global organization. Coordination refers to the extra tasks required for amalgamating tasks performed to accomplish the final goal, while collaboration deals with multiple teams working jointly toward the same objective. These two ingredients make a good virtual team, and in global organizations, more often than not, the teams are going to be virtual rather than physically sitting together. As a result, even the now well-known team building exercises take on a different meaning and format, requiring coordination and collaboration across time, space and cultural boundaries. In order to succeed in global coordination and collaboration, there is a need to establish common standards in terms of communication method, language, management rules, and

Figure 3.3. Four team organizational models of Thomsett (1994)

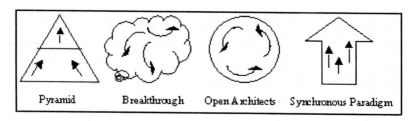

information technologies (as well as hardware platforms and software applications). In the context of global teams, if may be worth studying the four possible
team organizational models of Thomsett (1994) as shown in Figure 3.3. These
models – namely pyramid, breakthrough, open architects, and synchronous
paradigm – can be applied to global projects and global teams within the global
organizations. (Thomsett, 1994).

- Pyramid – has its roots in the industrial age. Projects are decomposed into
  functions, similar to how a business is decomposed into business functions, such as R&D, engineering, manufacturing, marketing, sales, distribution, accounting, and finance, with all the functions reporting to the same
  executive. A single person, the project manager, is responsible for the
  project and has the authority to make decisions. All team members are
  directly accountable to the project manager.

- Breakthrough – involves teams of random creatively independent staff.
  Team members do not wait for guidelines or directions, and have clear
  objectives in mind. For better performance, the breakthrough model
  requires freedom from interference, and freedom to investigate problems.
  This model is suggested for small-sized, short-term, and simple projects
  that do not require intensive coordination of interdependent units.

- Open architects – Members of this team model work collaboratively
  toward the project objectives. Functional roles are well defined in the
  team and rotated among team members. Software development teams are
  suggested to adopt the open architects model for making collaboration
  and consensus engineering more efficient and controllable (Constantine,
  1995).

- Synchronous paradigm – Team members share a common vision with the
  leader. The level of alignment with the common value and vision is the key

to eliminate tight control of any kind and increase the efforts made by each individual. Hence the leader of this team model has less workload in supervising and guiding the team members to carry out their responsibilities.

End-User Factors In Globalization

The end-users are the ultimate group of people using the global information systems on a regular basis. The task of managing and supporting end-user groups is not only in maintaining business information operations but is the key to evaluating and improving the global information systems. The fundamental concerns of the end-user management category in the globalization context (Lan, 2002) include managing end-user computing facilities, end-user computing education, introducing and learning new global information systems, help desk support, and end-user involvement in global information systems development as mentioned in the "Information Systems Effectiveness" section.

Managing End-User Computing Facilities

Controlling the end-user computing equipment and facilities is a complex assignment, especially in the global organization where business units are dispersed across nations. Managing end-user computing facilities should be taken into account when planning and designing the global information systems. Tasks involved in the end-user facilities management may include the identification of facilities in each of the business units and subsidiaries, verification of facilities availability, development of standard maintenance procedures, and the development of standard facility purchasing, logistic and distribution procedures.

Usability Issues in Global Information Systems (GIS)

Usability of information systems assumes key importance when organizations globalize. Usability can be understood as the ease with which users are able to use the software, as well as the value the software provides to them when they do their work. A highly significant aspect of usage-centered designs is the dialogue between the user and the designer through the medium of the user interface. In their discussion on the principles of usage-centered design, Constantine and Lockwood (1999) state:

> *"Effective user interface design is a dialogue - a dialogue between designers and users. The dialogue is founded on the realization that there are real people on the other side of the user interface and that good designs communicate effectively with them."*

The reason why this dialogue assumes greater importance in globalization is because of the fact that the user of the system (including customer and employees) may not be coming from a well–defined, socio-cultural-physical background. This means that people with different languages, colors and cultures, and different requirements will be accessing the global information systems, at the same time! It should be worth mentioning that while it is the software system and its interface that the user communicates with, behind that veneer lies the entire world of software projects including developers, managers, architects, testers and, of course, usage-centered designers. This requires careful attention to usage-centered design techniques including attention to user roles, tasks and user interface content, as discussed by Constantine and Lockwood (2002).

End-User Computing Education

In the modern business environment, employees' capabilities to use computers to perform business tasks seem to be part of the job requirements. The basic computing skills such as producing documents, sending e-mails, and browsing the Internet are required in most office environments. However, the level of employees' computing education in the global organization varies from subsidiary to subsidiary. Thus, there is a need to incorporate an end user computing education plan in the global transition process. The main objective of the plan is to ensure that the employees' have obtained the required computing skills in all business units. It may consist of the identification of the employees' current computing skills and levels, identification of essential computing skills development of training programs, and implementation of training programs.

Introducing and Learning Global Information Systems (GIS)

When the development of global information systems (GIS) reaches a certain level (such as the testing and deploying stages), training programs should be introduced. The training programs should be developed through the systems development teams and the human resources department collaboratively. In order to develop the appropriate training programs for the respective end-users, the initial stage is the mapping of the organizational hierarchy in terms of the end user types and their responsibilities to the system's functionality.

Help-Desk Support

As per many other business information systems, the help desk plays an important role in keeping the users satisfied when performing business tasks through the global information systems. To provide effective help-desk service, two fundamental concepts may be incorporated into the help-desk function – a clear understanding of what are the services the users anticipate, and accurately and in a timely fashion responding to problems reported by users. Figure 3.4 illustrates a proposed help-desk structure to accommodate the global information systems help services. It includes a centralized global end-user support center and various regional or local end-user support centers. The global end-user support center takes care of problems and requests dealing with trans-border activities in the global context and also manages the regional/local end-user support centers. In the regional/local centers, the main services are to firstly define the scope of request (global or regional/local) and secondly provide help on issues relating to local or regional activities. If the problem relates to the trans-border activities, the regional/local center will divert the request to the global end-user support center for resolution.

End-User Involvement in GIS Development

Users' perception and information requirements drive the entire development of the global information systems effort (Laudon & Laudon, 2002). Users must have sufficient control over the design and development of global information systems to ensure that business functions and operations are accurately

Figure 3.4. Global help-desk structure

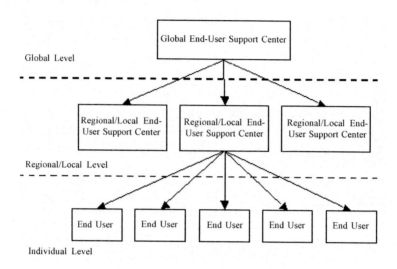

incorporated. Moreover, the design of global information systems should be based on all stakeholders. In other words, the lack of users' involvement in the design of global information systems is the major cause of systems failure.

There are always benefits associated with involving users as part of any information system development teams. However, it is even more important to engage users in the global information systems development. As mentioned above, users are people who understand the business functions and operations. Involving various types of users through the entire global information system analysis and design phases is crucial as it helps in making sure the global information system would appropriately implement business processes and bring extra value to the business. It is also believed that users who have been involved in the design and development phases would become change agents for the introduction of new systems. The change agents play the role of disseminating the concept of new systems to members in their local business unit and they may also be involved in developing training programs.

Cultural Factors In Globalization

When addressing information systems and technology globally, culture is an important aspect to be considered as it influences the success or failure of global transformation. In the new challenge of globalization the reality of cultural diversity is unavoidable. Organizations should be encouraged to embrace diversity and turn the multicultural characteristics into strategic advantages. Understanding this diversity is crucial to conducting any global business. As Kincaid (1999) correctly points out doing business "requires a deep respect of the country's culture, religions and institutions." Furthermore, understanding the cultural activities and variables will provide organizations with a certain level of competitive edge in the global business environment. O'Hara-Devereaux and Johansen (1994) introduced a multifaceted lens concept – a way of peering through the fog of cultural diversity. The multifaceted lens concept is based on the identification and understanding of various cultural dimensions including:

- Language – the vocabulary, structure, and meanings of oral and written communication. For example, a standardized global customer relationship management (CRM) application may require multiple interfaces designed in different language characters (such as English, Chinese, or Japanese) for subsidiaries in different countries. However, in a global organization it is very difficult for the internal communications to take place without an agreed common language.

- Context – the entire array of incentives surrounding every communication event. The measurement of context can be assigned either high or low. High-context cultures assign meaning to many of the incentives surrounding an unambiguous message. On the other hand, low-context cultures leave out many of those incentives and focus on the objective communication event (O'Hara-Devereaux and Johansen, 1994). For example, a high-context culture refers to an individual's "context" or their relationship with other people (e.g., families and friends) as more important (that is the "context" in which the individual relates to people/families) than the individuals themselves. Low-context culture means it is less important to whom an individual is related (i.e., the context in which the person operates), but more important what the individual does.

- Time – the concept of time and time management differ widely from culture to culture. As Hall and Hall (1990) described, cultural time differences can be thought of in either monochronic or polychronic categories. In the monochronic time category, people tend to do one single thing at a time. However, in the polychronic time category, people can perform multiple tasks at once. Another aspect in relation to time is orientation. Time orientations are generally partitioned as past, present and future. According to O'Hara-Devereaux and Johansen (1994), cultures are either future-oriented or past-oriented. Which means the current operations of business activities are designed to influence the future events or to be influenced by past events. Different cultures would have different emphasis on time orientation. For instance, Asian cultures are inclined to be oriented toward looking at a more distant future, than the immediate one. On the other hand, many Latin cultures are heavily influenced by the past. When planning for cross-culture collaborative works, for example the global information systems development teams with members across different nations and cultural backgrounds, organizations need to consider the employees' attitudes toward time categories and orientations and derive a balanced "time" solution for maximizing the performance in the global collaborative situation.

- Power equality – the degree of power and authority distribution and understanding of equality from different cultural perspectives. Organizational units in various cultures may have a diverse perception of power, authority, and equality among employees. For example, some cultures might demonstrate higher respect for professional, skilled employees than general, unskilled workers and thus skilled professionals would derive more power than unskilled workers. In this dimension, organizations ought to carefully adjust the power, authority, and equality given to employees in diverse cultural backgrounds while maintaining an equivalent level of distribution (power, authority, and equality) amongst business units.

- Information flow – the methods and paths of transferring information and data between people across levels and regions within the organization. Information flow is critical in productively carrying out business operations and achieving business objectives in a cross-cultural business environment. Global organizations need to realize the cultural impact on the information flow and ensure that information travels from one part of the organization to another within expected time, sequence, and format.

Additionally, many recent research publications have reported that the knowledge of culture and cultural environments is crucial for the success of the globalization process. In addition, a number of global information systems management activities related to culture and culture differences have been outlined by researchers (Burns et al., 1993; Ein-Dor, Segev and Orgad, 1993; Sauter, 1992; Yellen, 1997). These activities aim to draw the attention of organizations' intending to pursue globalization. There are several aspects pertaining to culture that need to be heeded by an organization planning to globalize its information systems management. These include education levels, geographical zones and time zones, religion, demographics, individual significance and objectives, communication, and leadership style. To recognize the importance of these, each aspect is further explored and discussed in the following sections.

Education Levels

The education level in relation to information technology and globalization depends upon various aspects of a country's vision. In some developing countries such as China and India, information technology seems to be the main agenda in the national education strategy as the rationale of competing with developed countries. However, some other countries have much less emphasis on information technology education. A company's transition to globalization can be impacted significantly based on the level of education in the regions it operates.

Geographical and Time Zones

Geographically dispersed business units with a range of time zones are characteristic of any organizations that operate business globally. This can be both helpful and detrimental. It can be helpful because of the round-the-clock information systems development scenario. On the other hand, the geographical and time zone differences could be detrimental. In video-conference and telephone conference situations, for instance, inter-organizational meetings scheduled at two o'clock in the afternoon in Sydney would cause difficulty for people to participate in New York (as it would be the middle of the night there).

Religion

Sometimes religion has a major influence on the daily schedule of business operations. For example, in the Islamic world, Friday is considered as the holy day and is part of the weekend instead of Sunday. Business units or subsidiaries in Islamic areas must align their business hours to the religious activities. Religious events also affect the organization's non-working (holiday) periods. For instance, most of the Western world has one week Christmas holiday. India is in holiday season during Diwali, somewhere in between the end October and early November; and the Arab countries and China will have different holiday periods. Organizations with business units or subsidiaries operating in different countries need to ensure that there are no scheduled business activities during the times and days for religious activities and festivals.

Demographic Perspective

The focus of the demographic aspect in the global culture category is specifically associated with the age and gender perspective. Age distribution can be quite different in every social culture. The general perceptions and values of age groups are also different from culture to culture. For example, many Western cultures value young people over their elders, whereas elders are revered in most Asian cultures. In the gender perspective, masculinity and femininity are the two key categories to be considered. In masculine cultures, gender roles are strictly delineated and conventional male values such as competitiveness and strength tend to be appreciated in organizations. In feminine cultures, stereotypical female values such as cooperation, caring and nurturing are valued and there is less demarcation between gender roles.

Although there is no perfect and standard solution to overcome the various cultural differences in age and gender aspects, organizations are strongly recommended to comprehend the meaning of these aspects in each culture and fine-tune the appropriateness to their working environment.

Significance and Objectives of the Individual

No matter where the employee is located, nor the position of the employee as a human being, an individual has his/her own objectives and outlook on life.

These objectives can be identified in three aspects: personal, social, and professional. From time to time, the emphasis of these aspects changes, or conflicts with each other. For instance, an individual's personal objective is to spend more time with the family, but a promotion opportunity is given to the individual with the condition of working several months overseas. Hence, the individual has to decide whether to take the promotion opportunity and sacrifice the family commitment. Similarly each organization has its own objectives and these objectives may conflict with employees' personal objectives. To overcome this conflict, the organizations must realize their employees' objectives, and negotiate with a realignment strategy to achieve a win-win situation.

Communication

As in the earlier discussion of O'Hara-Devereaux and Johansen's cultural lenses, communication primarily refers to languages in either verbal or written forms. Although English is the common language for business communication around the world in both written and verbal formats, there are other languages prominent in specific regions. For example, Chinese is the widespread language in the greater China region (including mainland China, Taiwan, Hong Kong, and Singapore). Spanish is the common language used in most Latin American countries. Adopting a language to be used across a multinational organization is a challenging task in the global transition process. In addition to language itself, methods used to send messages also play an import role in global business communication. The traditional ways of transferring messages amongst organizations are telephone conversations, faxes and telexes. On the other hand, e-mails, Web cam, and mobile SMS (Short Message Service) are the technological ways of transferring messages between companies.

Communication is always a major concern in most global organizations. Enterprises should ensure a standard communication typology is embedded in the policy and implemented in daily operations. The latest technologies relating to global business communication are discussed later in this chapter.

Environmental Factors in Globalization

Recently, many globalized organizations have demonstrated their successful business operations and improved overall efficiency over organizations which still remain locally focused. These global organizations extend across various industries such as IBM and Acer for the computer industry, Toyota and Ford for the automobile industry, McDonald's and Coca-Cola for the food industry, Bayer and Dupont for the chemical industry and Citibank for the banking industry (Moran & Riesenberger, 1996). To determine why globalized organizations possess more competitive strength over local organizations, certain factors should be investigated. These factors are used to provide certain fundamental concepts for the transition of business operations. These environmental factors can be further classified under two headings: proactive and reactive (Moran & Riesenberger, 1996).

Proactive Environmental Factors

In this class, organizations are proactive in determining the factors which will influence the transformation to globalization. These factors are global sourcing, continuous development of new markets, scales of economy, trends in product-service consistency, costs in global transportation, government regulations, telecommunications and equipment costs, and trends in technology standards. These are described in detail below.

Global Sources

In the competitive essence of the world trade activities, enterprises are searching for new sources of raw materials and components from everywhere and anywhere in the world. There are a number of elements, which would influence the enterprises' decision makers to shift their procurement origins from domestic to international suppliers. They are:

- Better quality.
- Lower costs.
- Better product technology.
- Distinction of technological services.

- Transportation speed.
- Demand satisfaction.
- Compelling competitive pressure to domestic suppliers.

New Markets

Continuously developed new markets provide opportunities to enterprise globalization.

Scale of Economy

Enterprises must find new competitive advantages in order to hold their market positions. Scale of economy is one of the ways to reduce the overall costs. When the production increases, the average production costs will be reduced.

Trend in Product-Service Consistency

The whole world's consumption trends have gradually changed from local or regional products to global products, such as McDonald's, Coca-Cola, consumer electronic products and Nike sportswear. These trends are caused by the diffusion of telecommunication and transportation. When customers grasp more global information, and face more and more diversified markets, the demand for product consistency and standardization is also increased. This kind of consistency demand will bring down the enterprises' inventory, purchasing and production costs, and advance their competitive advantages.

Lower Costs in Global Transportation

Costs of transportation in raw materials, components and finished products are some of the essential activities for the enterprise decision-maker in deciding whether overseas subsidiaries should exist. Some oversized or overweight components/finished products are required extremely costly to transport (sometimes the transportation costs may be higher than the actual cost of the goods). This is not an efficient way to transport products so they should be manufactured in the most appropriate global markets.

Government Regulation

In the last few decades, governments have always acted as protectors of domestic industries, and set up many trade obstacles as they still do now. These trade obstacles include tariff and non-tariff barriers. The purpose of these obstacles is to protect domestic social, political and economical benefits.

Tariff Barrier

Tariff refers to an additional tax charged on the product when it has arrived at or departed from a country's borders. The purpose of tariffs is usually to protect domestic industries or gain profit.

Basically, most governments agree that free trade would increase global competitiveness, and the result of this global competitiveness would assist in advancing a product's quality and decreasing the costs. Thus, the General Agreement on Tariffs and Trade (GATT) was founded after the World War II, and it functions to bring down or eliminate trade obstacles between countries, and press forward in free trading.

Non-Tariff Barrier

Many governments have also developed some sort of non-tariff obstacles to restrict or encourage the enterprises to export/import products to/from their countries. These non-tariff obstacles include voluntary export restraints (VERs), regulations for domestic marketplaces, dumping, domestic technical standards, government policies and export subsidies.

Lower Costs in Telecommunications and Equipment

Due to the rapid improvement in telecommunication equipment and the decrease of costs, many telephone companies provide low fees with high service standards. For this reason, enterprises are able to communicate with their foreign subsidiaries with almost real-time responses with limited overheads.

Trends in Technology Standards Consistency

Technology standards of consistency motivate suppliers to provide equal quality of products to consumers all over the world. For instance, ISO 90001 series standard (The International Organization for Standardization) is responsible for establishing global product quality standards. It provides guidelines to help the enterprises in the development of uniform production quality specifications.

Reactive Environmental Factors

In addition to the proactive environment factors, which drive globalization, there are some other threatening or reactive environment factors that could also influence enterprise to enter into globalization. These reactive environment factors can be classified in four classes: foreign competitors, increase of risks caused by exchange rate variation, the trend of expansion of customers from domestic to global markets, and rapid global technology transformation.

Foreign Competitors

Those enterprises that keep their business operations within their own country and do not intend to create foreign subsidiaries will suffer massive pressure from foreign competitors. The foreign competitors usually exist in three situations:

- Importing new products.
- Developing new competitive products by the alliance of foreign and domestic competitors.
- Foreign enterprises incorporating domestic competitors.

The above three situations will place the domestic enterprise in a highly disadvantaged position. These new competitors (foreign competitors) possess many more competitive advantages than domestic competitors. They are: having a pathway to gain the latest global technology, scope of economy, searching globally for raw materials and labor, forming alliances with domestic enterprises to decrease or even eliminate business obstacles, and sharing of development knowledge from global subsidiaries.

Increasing of Risks Caused by Exchange Rate Variation

The variation of market exchange rates would seriously affect the enterprise's profit. When the enterprise deals with foreign suppliers, the payment method and terms should be discussed before the order is completed, because the longer the term of payment, the higher risk the exchange rate variation. Purchasing staff in the enterprise should also have enough skills and understanding of the variation of exchange rates when they decide to deal with foreign suppliers.

The Trend of Expansion of Customers from Domestic to Global Markets

The strategy of business operations focuses on the domestic market to ensure the existing and potential customers only purchase domestically produced goods or services. When the customers are already in the globalization processes or in the situation of global searching for sources, the domestic enterprises would probably lose these customers if they did not consider creating foreign subsidiaries to support the customer requirements.

Rapid Global Technology Transformation

Since the early 1980s, new technology fast progress has had an influenced on enterprise profit and operations. Improvement of production procedure has caused the restructuring of the enterprise's market share. More and more enterprises have invested in the research and development field, and have employed these latest technologies to develop better ideas and products that will make a fortune for the enterprise.

The influences and transformation degree of the above twelve environmental factors enforce the faster processes of enterprise globalization. The enterprises with the majority of business activity in the domestic market are facing competitive pressure form overseas; however, global enterprises are also struggling in the extreme competitive environment for their survival.

In order to survive in the global business environment, the enterprises must carefully evaluate these environment factors and analyze current and future foreseeable influences and trends. This procedure also leads the enterprises in the development of global strategic vision.

Technology Factors in Globalization

Technologies are considered the main driver of making the global enterprise transition possible. As the rapid development of the information and communication technologies, we have highlighted a number of the enabling technologies for enterprises pursuing globalization. These latest enabling technologies include the Internet technologies, the Extranets and the Intranets, Middleware, Web Services, Groupware, Mobile technology and IT Architecture, and we discuss these technologies in detail in Chapter V.

Summary

In this chapter, we discussed the framework for enterprise globalization. The framework highlighted the need for detailed planning, preparation, and investigation of activities before the implementation of global transition processes can take place. In order to provide a clear understanding of concerns in global transition, six categories of transition activities are identified. These were: business, human resources, end-users, cultural, environmental, and technology. Each of these categories and their corresponding factors are further explored and discussed. Some suggestions and recommendations are proposed to manage these factors. Based on this understanding of the vision, process and framework for GET, we are now ready to consider enactment of the GET process in practice in the next chapter.

References

Burn et al. (1993). Critical issues of IS management in Hong Kong: A cultural comparison. *Journal of Global Information Management, 1*(4), 28-37.

Clikeman, P. (1999). Improving information quality. *Internal Auditor*.

Constantine, L.L. (1995). *Constantine on peopleware* (p. 84). NJ: Prentice Hall.

Constantine, L.L., & Lockwood, L.A.D. (1999). *Software for use: A practical guide to the models and methods of usage centered design* (p. 41). Reading, MA: Addison-Wesley.

Constantine, L.L., & Lockwood, L.A.D. (2002, March/April). Usage-centered engineering for Web applications. *IEEE Software, 19*(2), 42-50.

Ein-Dor, P., Segev, E., & Orgad, M. (1993). The effect of national culture on IS: Implications for international information systems. *Journal of Global Information Management, 1*(1), 33-44.

English, L.P. (2001). Information quality management: The next frontier. *Annual Quality Congress Proceedings, Milwaukee, pp.529-533.*

Gates, B. (1999). *Business @ the speed of though: Using a digital nervous system* (p.14-15). England: Penguin Books.

Hall, E.T., & Hall, M.R. (1990). *Understanding cultural differences: Germans, French, and Americans* (p.16). Yarmouth, Maine: International Cultural Press.

Hammer, M., & Stanton, S.A. (1995). *The reengineering revolution* (p. 3). MA: Harvard Business School.

Jones, S. (2001). Going global: How international firms are using the Internet to recruit. *Canadian HR Reporter, 14*(21), 21.

Kincaide, J. (1999, February). A CT passage to India. *Computer Telephony*, 100-114.

Lan, Y. (2002). GISM issues for successful management of the globalisation process. *Proceedings of the Third Annual Global Information Technology Management World Conference*, pp.224-227.

Laudon, K.C., & Laudon, J.P. (1993). *Business information systems: A problem-solving approach* (2nd ed.). FL: Dryden Press, Harcourt Brace & Company, p. 5.

Leontiades, J.C. (2001). *Managing the global enterprise* (pp.58-65). London: Pearson Education.

Moran, R.T., & Riesenberger, J.R. (1996). *The global challenge: building the new worldwide enterprise*. UK: McGraw-Hill.

O'Hara-Devereaux, M., & Johansen, R. (1994). *Globalwork: bridging distance, culture, and time*. CA: Jossey-Bass.

Palvia, S., & Saraswat, S.P. (1992). Information technology and the transnational corporation: The emerging multinational issues. In S. Palvia, P. Palvia, & R. Zigli (Eds.), *The global issues of information technology management*. Hershey, PA: Idea Group.

Porter, M.E. (1998). *On competition* (pp.166-167). MA: Harvard Business School.

Sauter, V.L. (1992). Cross-cultural aspects of model management needs in a transnational decision support system. In S. Palvia, P. Palvia, & R. M. Zigli (Eds.), *The global issues of information technology management*. Hershey, PA: Idea Group.

Senn, J. (1992). Assessing the impact of western Europe unification in 1992: Implications for corporate IT strategies. In S. Palvia, P. Palvia, & R. M. Zigli (Eds.), *The global issues of information technology management*. Hershey, PA: Idea Group.

Thomsett, R. (1994, December). When the rubber hits the road: A guide to implementing self-managing teams. *American Programmer*, 37-45.

Unhelkar, B. (2002). *Process quality assurance for UML-based projects*. MA: Addison-Wesley.

Yellen, R.E. (1997). End user computing in a global environment. *Journal of End User Computing, 9*(2), 33-34.

Endnotes

[1]   ISO 9000 index, International Organization for Standardization. Retrieved June 14, 2001 from the World Wide Web at: *http://www.iso.org/iso/en/iso9000-14000/iso9000/iso9000index.html*

Chapter IV

Enacting Global Enterprise Transitions

In this chapter we discuss:

- Enacting, in practice, the Global Enterprise Transitions (GET)
- Formally launching the transition
- Managing the human resources, time and budgets in practice
- Training, knowledge dissipation and change management in practice
- Measuring the process of GET during enactment
- Discuss practical tips and guidance relevant to GET in practice
- Verification of successful, practical GET
- Quality aspects in practical GET

Enactment is the application of the theory of the Global Enterprise Transition (GET) process *in practice*. Thus, while the discussion up to the previous chapter in this book may be considered akin to a roadmap, the discussion here is more like *actual driving* on the road. Figure 4.1 explains the subtle differences between enactment and the earlier works an organization undertakes during the globalization process.

In Figure 4.1, the "Consider GET" phase indicates that the organization is investigating and weighing various options, issues and factors in terms of globalization. These options and factors were considered in detail in Chapter I. As described earlier, this is the state when the organization realizes that irrespective of its current profitability and position in the market, globalization is becoming a serious part of its business strategy for survival and growth. Once the organization is satisfied and its stakeholders are convinced of the need to globalize, it then moves into the phase of "Planning and Documenting the GET process" as shown in Figure 4.1. During this phase, the organization is again applying the discussions undertaken so far in this book, particularly Chapters II and III, which encompass the vision, framework and technologies for global enterprise transitions. These visions and frameworks provide the backdrop for the planning and documentation activities that described the GETs. The organization may be considered in a strategic mode thus far. However, once the strategic aspect of the GET is consummated, the very practical phase of the process — the launching and management of the GET begins. These are the third and fourth states in which the organization finds itself, together called "Enactment," as shown in Figure 4.1. With the commencement of this practical enactment phase of the GET, various additional and valuable activities like handling the "feedback" from the stakeholders in terms of the efficacy of the process of GET, mechanisms to manage the process in practice and approach to measuring the results of the GET, all come into play. It is this practical phase

Figure 4.1. Global enterprise transition in practice

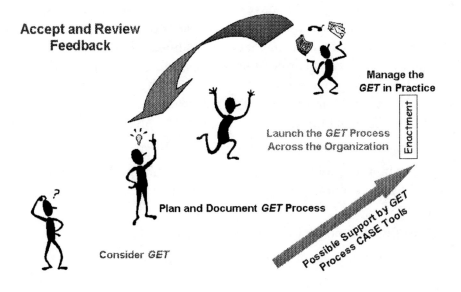

of the transition that forms the crux of this Chapter IV. In terms of the aforementioned roadmap analogy, it can be said that just as the same roadmap can be followed in different ways to reach the same destination, similarly the GET process may also be enacted in different ways depending, amongst other factors, on the state of preparedness of the organization and the actual "driving conditions" (based on discussions by Unhelkar and Mamdapur, 1995). The need for continuous feedback and acting on the feedback is as important in a GET enactment as in driving a vehicle. Discussions on these significant aspects of enactment follow.

Enactment: Transition in Practice

Enactment of the GET process moves the organization from theory to practice, bringing into play the dynamics and the unknowns of globalization. This requires careful management of all practical aspects of the transition project including people, processes and technologies – the latter involving development and implementation of software systems. Thus, the skills and acumen of the people and teams in charge of these transitions become significant during this GET enactment. The earlier planning framework outlined in this book may be considered necessary for globalization, but it is certainly not sufficient. It is the ensuing enactment that makes the planning and documentation of the GET real. The enactment of the global transition is execution of a sophisticated project that involves enormous skills and resources from all parts of the organization. This requires each phase of the transition partitioned into small chunks of activities that can be easily managed, measured and assessed through the appropriate measurement protocols at predetermined checkpoints. The measurements will also provide information on the quality of the transition process as well as the success, or lack thereof, of the resultant global organization. The overall activities that form part of the enactment involve the following:

- Launching the global transition – in itself a senior management responsibility and a separate and substantial chunk of the enactment part of the process
- Ensuring that the GET process plan is being followed in practice
- Keeping executive consensus during the GET

- Managing resources – including human and infrastructural resources
- Managing time and budgets
- Deploying the organization's units or alliances in foreign markets
- Training and knowledge dissipation
- Change management
- Reviewing and feedback mechanisms
- Verifying the efficacy of the transitions

These significant and practical aspects of GET, under the umbrella of enactment, are now discussed in greater detail.

Launching the Global Transition

The very first practical aspect of enacting the globalization process is the launching of the process. This is the first "external" announcement by the organization that it is going global. The work done so far on the GET framework, in terms of preparedness, planning and documentation is an invaluable starting point for enactment. During this early part of the enactment, the various socio-cultural-political aspects of globalization come into practice. This requires getting the external parties including employees, customers and business partners involved in the globalization process. Proper launch of the GET process will help in enticing this involvement from the external parties. And this involvement is important as, with GET enactment, the structure and behavior of the globalizing organization is bound to change – in turn affecting all internal and external parties that deal with the organization. And without their involvement and participation in the GET process during enactment, that enactment will not succeed. Due to the sheer importance of the launch, it is advisable to launch the transition through a steering committee, which is made up of various significant roles within the organization. While the exact composition of the committee can vary for different organizations, it is vital to include in the committee, customer representatives as well as representatives from business partners that will be affected by this transition. The timing of the launch of the global transition is also crucial and it depends upon the existing environmental situation including the current business, political and financial situation. In fact, during the launch, the organization moves into the mode of checking and re-checking the effect the transition is going to have on these partners as it moves forward with globalization. The launch, being the first step taken during enactment, plays an essential part in ensuring that the actual transition is as smooth as possible.

Following the GET Process Plan

With the launch of the GET process, the organization moves rapidly into the real implementation phase of GET. One of the practical risks that arise during the implementation is the possibility of the enactment going astray from the planned and documented GET. Therefore, during enactment, it is vital to follow the process and accompanying plans created thus far. Following the plan is a significant part of enactment, because GET is not a simple project that can be enacted out of a manager's "mind." During globalization, the organization has to go beyond not only its current business, but also its geo-political comfort zone. This produces eventualities that may be confusing, surprising and not fully understood and documented. Following the process during practical enactment of GET is of great assistance as it helps in reducing the "surprise element" in terms of the human resources and management operations which may all appear differently in practice even if they have been considered during the planning phase. Thus, following a plan may be considered as one of the significant risk reduction techniques during enactment. Enactment reveals areas where the organization needs to find out more, and the transition plan continues to provide the organization with a roadmap to follow during the enactment. Finally, following a plan is helpful in global IT transition as it enables the enacting organization to avoid major conflicts with external parties, unexpected shortages of resources and budgets and understanding the feedback during the transition. Generally, the planning process and the following of the plan during enactment are closely tied to each other, and to the success of the GET.

Keeping Executive Consensus

Further to the need to follow the plan, another major non-technical issue that needs to be handled during enactment is maintenance of complete executive consensus. This is vital to enactment as, without consensus and support from the executive cadres of the organization, the entire GET process has the potential to fail in practice. In addition to subscribing to the globalization process, it is imperative that the decision makers of the organization have a clear understanding of the globalization strategy and have recognized the implications of enacting the global transition process. Lack of this understanding and the resultant discord is one of the highest risks to the globalizing organization. While numerous practical project management activities can help in maintaining this consensus and understanding, the following four activities are specifically recommended during GET enactment:

- Communicating with internal employees and external business partners such as suppliers and customers about the organization's steps in going global and how this globalization affecting them in the immediate and distant future. Both electronic and physical communications, including physical meetings, is highly recommended during the early enactment phase.

- Organizing regular management reviews by the steering committee to ensure that the GET process itself has been kept updated, publicized and recognized by the organization as a whole.

- Keeping the company's stated mission, objectives, quality policies and related documents "current" and publicized both physically, electronically and by "word of mouth" over the grapevine, as the GET process is enacted.

- Keeping the line of authority and responsibilities of all parties concerned clearly delineated and publicized. This is crucial as, in the GET process, people from different organizations will be involved; and the culture and value systems of the organizations and the societies within which these organizations exist can create friction and discontent, if not properly stated, understood and adhered to.

Managing Resources

Lan (2003) has listed three major categories of resources that should be made available in a timely fashion during GET enactment. They are people (as human resources), information, and infrastructure (both business and technology) resources. These three categories of resources are the essential and critical components in the company's global transition project and they are further expanded next.

- *People* – or human resources (HR) are one of the most important aspects of any project. However, because of the cross-cultural differences that exist between different geo-political regions that the globalizing organization has to traverse, these human factors assume phenomenal importance (Unhelkar, 2003). It is imperative during the enactment of GET that there is sufficient "buy in" from employees, customers and personnel from the external organizations with which alliances may have been formed. Timely availability, skills and commitment of human resources is vital for the success of the enactment. More specifically, though, the people that play a major role in a GET enactment are the employees who are directly or indirectly involved in the company's global IT transition project. There are three types of operations staff who will be involved during the GET enactment. Firstly, the CEO and the Senior Managers (typically members of the steering committee) will be involved in establishment of a global e-business alliances (see Chapter 1, for discussions on e-business alliances) or a corresponding foreign subsidiary. After such alliances and/or subsidiaries have been established, the "operational personnel" will be involved in the enactment of transition. These involve roles like the vice president, production manager, chief engineer and finance manager – those who look after the actual production or service processes in the newly established foreign presence. It is worth re-iterating here the fact that despite the electronic capabilities of the Internet providing the backbone for GETs, it is still essential to consider these "physical" (or non-electronic) aspects of the globalization process to ensure its success. Finally, when it comes to deployment of corresponding global information systems in the process of GET, it is essential to consider the technical roles required such as analysts, programmers, database managers and testers, to name but a few.

- *Information* – this refers to all the informative resources needed during enactment and include the data and information about our own organization as well as the external environment into which it is expanding. For example, the informative resources may include the investigation report of foreign markets, the estimated foreign subsidiary's monthly total products manufactured and the labor costs of the foreign subsidiary. Furthermore, relevant quality, standards, legal and political data and information, being made available in both paper and electronic forms, are invaluable resources during GET enactment. Although it is important to glean this information during the earlier planning stages, the importance of latest and most current information during enactment cannot be overemphasized.

- *Infrastructure* – this is the non-personnel resource that primarily refers to both business and technology infrastructure that is required to be deployed during enactment. For example, for a product-based organization, infrastructure resources include production machinery, engineering and mechanical equipment, delivery trucks, raw material areas, semi-product areas, final product areas, storage areas and packaging areas. For a service-based organization, the infrastructure is relatively less physical, but still requires the necessary basis for delivery of the service. For example, a call center service going global will have to establish or upgrade its infrastructure to provide for the needs of a global organization, as against the earlier localized organization. Furthermore, from a physical infrastructure viewpoint, all organizations may need resources such as phones and faxes, computer servers and workstations, computer peripherals (printers, scanners), network components (hubs, routers and cables), and backup equipment.

Managing Time and Budgets

Enactment brings to life the major constraints of time and budget in practice. While a thorough project plan requires incorporating the management of company resources, time and cost towards the completion of all project activities (Kerzner, 2001), it is the practical aspect of monitoring that time and budget that requires the attention of the team in charge of the GET. Usually, a global transition process is considered a comparatively large project in terms of time, cost and resources. Without careful and continuous monitoring of the time and cost, such projects with a global focus will have possibilities of failure despite excellent planning. Furthermore, the timing and budgets need continuous "revisions" based on the time and money spent "thus far" in order to keep these factors on track during GET. Finally, due to the involvement of numerous external parties and possible alliances during GET, it is essential to update all these parties in terms of the time and budgets relevant to them.

Deploying in Foreign Markets

The key difference between a Global and Non-Global organization is the presence of foreign business units. Thus, usually, the GET process will lead organizations to the establishment of foreign subsidiaries or business units.

Therefore, during enactment, it is crucial to understand the intended foreign markets as early as possible before establishing the business units or subsidiaries. This understanding should not be concentrated merely on the sales potential for the market. Instead, it should comprehensively cover every aspect of the market such as the freedom of fund flows, taxation systems, employees' knowledge level, labor costs, effective distribution channels, telecommunication infrastructure, culture, political situation, encouragement of foreign investment, public order and human rights. While a part of this investigation is undertaken during the earlier planning stages of GET, it is during enactment that this takes on a very practical meaning. Since the foreign markets and their conditions are likely to change *continuously,* it is essential to continue to monitor the market conditions where globalization is likely to take place first. Thus, the evaluation of these factors should not be restricted to the current time and place; in fact it is more appropriate to deliberate over these factors for relatively longer periods of time (say five years). In other words, the measurement of appropriateness should be focused on both current and long-term business operations. A list of these foreign factors in GET enactment is provided in Table 4.1, for an organization that used it for its GET to China. The appropriateness level, shown here with a tick, may be extended and made more comprehensive to include percentages and weighting to arrive at the impact of these factors on GET.

In the early stages of investigating these factors, organizations would spend the majority of the time collecting foreign market information and analyzing

Table 4.1. Example foreign market measurements during enactment of a GET

Candidate City – Guangzhou, China			
"Foreign factors" influencing GET of organization "XYZ"	Appropriateness Level (%ages may be used)		
	Low	Medium	High
Freedom of fund flows		✓	
Taxation systems	✓		
Employees' knowledge level		✓	
Labor costs			✓
Effective distribution channels		✓	
Telecommunication infrastructure	✓		
Culture			✓
Political situation			✓
Encouragement of foreign investment		✓	
Public order	✓		
Human rights	✓		

appropriate locations for overseas business operations. These activities are mainly initiated by the chief executive officer or senior managers who have been appointed to be involved in the management of the global transition process.

In the second stage, the transition activities focus on the establishment of global business units. Establishing foreign business units is a complicated task. In order to ensure the successful establishment of overseas business units, it is crucial that the parent company is effectively providing necessary resources and support. Senior managers and middle-level managers who have the knowledge of local markets and foreign businesses' operating capability are the most appropriate candidates at this stage.

The third stage is the implementation or operation of the global transition stage. Activities at this stage rely on the specific business functions assigned to the business unit. For instance, if the foreign business unit is to conduct production activities, then the implementation of the global operation would be based on performing production-related tasks such as the purchases of materials, stock and inventory management, the manufacturing process, the quality control process, the packaging process, and the distribution and delivery operations. Consequently, the HR department is intensively involved in this stage to ensure that sufficient resources are available for perpetual implementation.

Finally, the activities related to deployment in foreign markets may further benefit by the application of information and communications technologies, through software systems. For example, data collected in stage one can be centralized in a database management system, which would be employed as the information source for other information system components to provide further analysis to the organization. During enactment, intensive data and information are flowing between the parent company and the overseas business unit. To perform an effective data transferring process, both sites (the parent company and the foreign business unit) should construct equivalent information technology architecture (discussed in Chapter V). Such IT architecture should have the capability to cope with heavy data traffic and be available at all times.

Training and Knowledge Dissipation

The globalization process changes the way in which various stakeholders interact with the organization. Especially, an electronic global organization ends up redefining its relationship with its employees, customers, business partners, and the government. It may be reiterated here that the globalized organization is not merely an "automated" organization, but an organization with characteristics, features and opportunities unique to an electronic organization. This requires the organization to ensure that the various participants it used to interact with are now made aware of the new protocols and procedures (which may be hopefully simpler, easier and cheaper) on those interactions. This is where training and knowledge dissipation comes into the picture.

Ideally, training the employees, customers, suppliers and other partners should form a separate and dedicated area of global enterprise transition. It should have a separate budget during transition, and should be made the responsibility of a specific team or person responsible for the transition project or its quality. Typically, the training aspect of GET in practice should encompass the following:

- Identification of a target audience for the training.

- Incorporation of new rules and regulations, procedures and protocols in the electronic aspect of the organization.

- Plan for hands-on training, as the users use the software to interact with the organization.

- Training in software products that will be used in global interactions.

- Training and guidance in terms of handling the changing socio-political situation resulting from the globalization of the organization.

Change Management in Practice

As the GET process commences, it will change both the structure and dynamics of the organization. The customer, supplier, employees, management and government are the candidate entities which will undergo change in their relationships with the organization. Firstly, this will involve changes to the way the people and processes were organized. Concept of business process reengineering (BPR) and business process modeling (BPM) and the way the changes are handled in organizations when BPR/BPM is brought about will be relevant. Secondly, the way in which the organization interacts with its external business partners and internally with its customers, will change primarily based on the technology. A globalized organization will be keen to switch most of the interactions to *electronic* interactions, as it will be dealing with large distances and different time zones for conducting its business operations. This will require documentation of newer processes, procedures for setting up and carrying out interactions, and mechanisms to handle security and privacy issues. It is suggested that during GET, changes to technology, people and processes are handled in this sequence.

Reviewing and Feedback

Feedback is vital to the success of GET process in practice. Also, it is worth mentioning that feedback comes into play only during enactment, and not before. Once the GET process is launched, mechanisms should be put in place to encourage participants to provide feedback. This feedback can be in the form of electronic feedback, paper-based comments, verbal messages, and so on. Non-specific feedback, coming from the informal views expressed by participants in the GET process should also be considered. Constant feedback for the global transition process provides organizations with opportunities to identify significant issues, which, if left unattended, may cause failure of the entire project. The feedback would allow organizations to quickly respond to the problems and assure the transition activities are conducted accurately. Feedback also creates a "buy-in" for the people, and their feeling of involvement is crucial to the GET process. Generally, feedback originates from people who have the association or involvement with the transition project. These people may be spread across the entire organization and may be able to provide valuable feedback regardless of their physical locations or the level of authority. For instance, they could be senior managers who are deeply involved in the global transition process, or a local order entry operator who wishes to provide comments on the global information systems as it affects her work in the new global environment. Additionally, feedback from independent parties would also provide the organization with invaluable information on the effect GET is having on their interactions with the organization. Ensuring following of standards, "local" rules and regulations, and understanding "local" protocols, are all important results of reviews and feedback. The reviews and feedback coming externally, from the organization's suppliers and customers, may help alleviate concerns about the effectiveness of the organization's global operations in association with their business activities and competitive advantages.

Finally, the GET process itself may be subjected to reviews and feedback to enhance its enactment. For example, the well known techniques of internal audits and reviews may be used to document the steps, time and expenses for each of the transition activities and tasks. Once the data is recorded, it can then be used to verify if the process has satisfied the requirements of the quality standards (such as ISO9001 or CMM-i) being applied to the project.

Verifying Global Enterprise Transitions

During the global transition process, it is crucial that organizations are aware of the progress and levels of achievement through a measurable topology. By following the GET, organizations become capable of determining their stages and achievements in the globalization process across all business functions. Verification of GET means evaluating and determining whether the organization has achieved its globalization objectives. There are three significant reasons for this: Firstly, the purpose of the measurement is to help the company understand basic behaviors of the changing business and its system, especially in relationships with other businesses and systems it is dealing with. Secondly, the purpose of such verifications is to evaluate the status of the enactment of the GET process and how it correlates to the initial project plan. Thus, these evaluations help in judging the progress of the project and its value to the corporate strategic goals stated at the beginning of the project. Thirdly, and finally, these verifications lead to opportunities for future improvement in the process of transitions.

A formal and appropriate global transition measurement will provide the mechanism for this verification process. Such appropriate and precise measurements for evaluating the company's global achievement can only be had through a corresponding systematic model.

In order to construct such appropriate and precise measurements for evaluating the company's global achievement, it is crucial to develop the measurement model in a systematic manner. Generally, the measurement model development starts with determining what to measure. In the context of globalization, the objects to be measured are the five global transition issue categories (business, human resources, technology, end user, and cultural) identified in Chapter III. However, due to the broad coverage of individual categories, each of these categories is further broken down into subcategories. Based on the six core categories, we have identified 18 subcategories and they are referred to as the measuring factors.

Table 4.2. Indication of achievement level

Measurement Block	Percentage of achievement
0	0 – 10 %
1	11 – 20 %
2	21 – 30 %
3	31 – 40 %
4	41 – 50 %
5	51 – 60 %
6	61 – 70 %
7	71 – 80 %
8	81 – 90 %
9	91 – 100 %

The second step of the model development deals with defining measurement criteria. Based on the definition of each factor (subcategory), numerous issues can be identified and transformed into the measurement criteria, which the organizations have to accommodate during the process of global transition. Consequently, a measurement technique should be designed to assess these criteria. In this study, the measurement technique is designed as a 100 percent scale, which is partitioned into ten measurement blocks and illustrated in Table 4. 2.

Once the measurement objects and the criteria and measuring technique are defined, the measurement model is ready in its implementation position. Each of Tables 4.3 through 4.7 contain the measurement criteria of an issue category, a list of measuring factors, the associated measuring criteria and the sample measurement results.

After the evaluation, a calculation mechanism should be applied to reach a conclusion about the globalization achievement. This calculation mechanism is described as follows. The first calculation item is the achievement of each measurement factor. It is derived from the average of the associated measuring criteria. For example, in Table 4.3 the "strategic planning" (the measurement factor) consists of three measuring criteria (1-3), and their measured results are 9, 8, and 8 respectively. Thus the achievement level of "strategic planning" is 8.3 (or 83% as in Table 4.2). After the achievement levels of all measurement factors are determined, each GISM issue category can be evaluated. Once again, this is calculated from the average of associated measurement factors. From the "human resources" achievement evaluation table (Table 4.4), the achievement level is calculated from the average of three measurement factors which are the role of senior management: 7, staff recruitment and training: 7.3,

Table 4.3. Measurement criteria for business category

Category 1: Business	Measuring Scale 0 - 9
Strategic planning	
Applying information systems for global business opportunities and competitive advantage	9
Alignment of information systems and business objectives	8
Understanding of information systems roles, contribution and justification of information systems investments	8
Reengineering and change	
Business processes are reengineered through the adoption of IT	8
Developing necessary procedures and programs for managing business reengineering changes	8
Applying a quality assurance scheme for organizational management	9
IT professionals possess business-oriented competence when developing global information systems	7
Managing IT quality	
The global information system is reliable, available and transferable within the organization	7
Applying appropriate quality control mechanisms for inputs and outputs of information systems	8
Applying software quality assurance standards in the development and maintenance of global information systems	8
Productivity	
Developing an appropriate measurement and improvement of information system productivity and effectiveness	8
Full utilization of data resources	7
Systems development and implementation	
The new global information system has been constructed, implemented and managed	7
Implementing office automation	9

Table 4.4. Measurement criteria for human resources category

Category 2: Human Resources	Measuring Scale 0 - 9
Role of senior management	
Possessing quality skills in people management	8
Developing training programs for senior management in IS and cross-cultural skills	6
Staff recruitment and training	
Retaining, recruiting, and training IT personnel	7
Sufficiency and availability of IT staff	6
Organizing and managing expatriated employees and assignments	9
Benefits and compensation	
Incorporating multinational compensation schemes into the company's policy	9
Company's travel activities are minimized to reduce unnecessary costs	6

Table 4.5. Measurement criteria for technology category

Category 3: Technology	Measuring Scale 0 - 9
IT infrastructure	
Appropriate computer hardware and operating systems have been selected and the management and support procedures are clearly outlined	9
Business applications	
Appropriate software applications have been identified, constructed, implemented, and managed	7
Information systems are integrated across all business functions	7
Telecommunications network	
Appropriate management, planning, support, and availability of telecommunications infrastructure and technology	7
Data and information systems improvement	
Procedures for continuous improvement of data, information and knowledge quality	6
Developing security, control, and disaster recovery capabilities	7
Integration of databases for data mining ability	7

Table 4.6. Measurement criteria for end user category

Category 4: End User	Measuring Scale 0 - 9
Organizational learning	
Procedures for facilitation and management of organizational learning	8
Enhancing staff absorption of the new information systems	8
Procedures and facilities for end user computing	8
Operation and support	
Procedures for managing IT operations	9
Developing help desk support	7

Table 4.7. Measurement criteria for cultural category

Category 5: Cultural	Measuring Scale 0 - 9
Education	
Investigation of the level of general education of people in the region or nation	6
Investigation of the level of computer knowledge of people in the region or nation	7
Demographics	
Investigation of regional or national gender perspective	6
Investigation of age distribution of the region or nation	6
Investigation of regional or national religion	6
Individual and interpersonal perspectives	
Investigation of leadership style of the region or nation	6
Investigation of values and goals of individuals and groups of the region or nation	7
Investigation of interpersonal communications of the region or nation	7
Geography and economy	
Investigation of currency stability	8
Coping with time-zone difference	8

Table 4.8. Level of GET achievement

GISM Issues Category	Level of GET Achievement
Business	79%
Human Resources	73%
End User	80%
Technology	74%
Cultural	68%

and benefits and compensation: 7.5. Hence, the achievement level of the "human resources" category is 7.3 (or 73% as in Table 4.2).

Based on the sample measurement results, the Table 4.8 presents the achievement level of the GET process in five categories.

The measured results do not merely indicate the company's achievement level in globalization, they also specify the less emphasized aspects, which the company has to pay more attention to for future improvement. To generalize the above measurement procedures, a conceptual model for measuring global IT transition achievement is developed, which is illustrated in Figure 4.2 and described as follows.

The conceptual model of globalization achievement measurement is constructed as a top-down decomposition of hierarchical structure. This hierarchical structure allows organizations to view their globalization achievement in four levels, including the entire organization level, main GISM issues category level, GISM issues subcategory level, and measuring criteria level. The highest level represents the globalization achievement of the entire organization. The result of this level would provide senior executives with an abstract view of what is the company's status and achievement of the global transition process. This organization level is based on the amalgamation of the second level – the main GISM issues category level components. It consists of the measurement of the five main global information systems management issues categories defined earlier. Each of these five is further broken into a number of subcategories, which form the third level. For example, the "business" category in the second level of the hierarchy is divided into five subcategories containing strategic planning, reengineering and change, managing IT quality, productivity, systems development and implementation, which form the third level. Furthermore, the bottom level represents a range of validating criteria that are identified and applied for the measurement of each subcategory.

Figure 4.2. Conceptual model of globalization achievement measurement

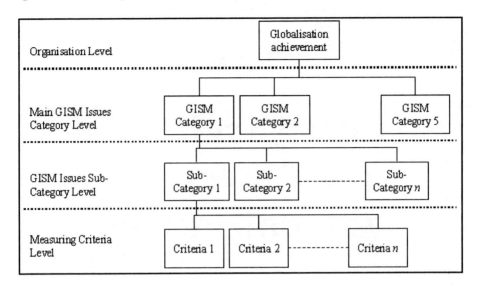

Summary

In this chapter, we discussed the enactment of the GET process. Enactment brings in all the practical aspects of GET. This discussion is essential as the organization moves from the planning and envisioning phase to the practical phase. A number of practical factors that affect the enactment were discussed. These included the launching of the project, its management, its deployment across foreign shores, training, reviews and feedback. Although these are fairly comprehensive factors, it is expected that more factors will be encountered during various specific enactments by organizations.

References

Lan, Y., & Khan, K. (2003). Measuring the readiness of globalisation: A metrics based approach. *Proceedings of Information Resources Management Association International Conference*, pp. 723-726.

Unhelkar, B., & Mamdapur, G. (1995). Practical aspects of using a methodology: A road map approach. *Report on object analysis and design (ROAD), 2*(2), 34-36, 54.

Chapter V

Enabling Technologies for Enterprise Globalizations

In this chapter we discuss:

- Role of enabling technologies in Global Enterprise Transitions
- Internet technologies, their accessibility and relevance in Global Business
- Web services: XML, SOAP, WSDL, UDDI in the context of Global Business
- Middleware (CORBA, DCOM), Groupware and IT Architecture

Introduction

We have discussed, thus far, the vision of a global enterprise and the process of achieving that vision. However, it is the technologies available today that have made such globalization possible. In this chapter, we deepen our understanding of globalization by delving into the technologies that facilitate this globalization. In addition to the technically minded reader, this understanding will be helpful to the business reader in correlating the technologies that bring about these transitions. At the outset, it is crucial to understand that the fundamental basis of these technologies is their ability to facilitate communication electronically. Figure 5.1 shows these *enabling technologies*: Internet

Figure 5.1. The enabling technologies of Global Enterprise Transitions (GET)

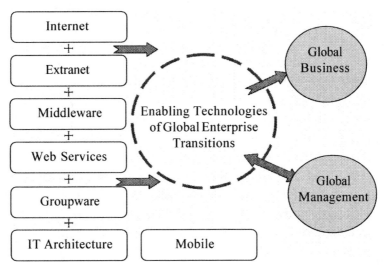

technologies, Extranets and Intranets, Middleware, Web Services, Groupware and an overall framework of IT Architecture that encompasses functional, network, software and security architecture. These technologies, forming the backbone of IT communication, influence and are influenced by mobile technologies which, together with Web Services, are categorized under Emerging Technologies. These technologies are enablers and drivers of the process of transitioning to global enterprises, as shown in Figure 5.1. Furthermore, they also impact Global IT Management. It is essential that we discuss these enabling technologies within the context of Global Enterprise Transitions (GET), as is done in this chapter.

Enabling Technologies: Synopsis

This discussion of enabling technologies for GET starts with a synopsis of these technologies. These technologies extend the definition of an information system as given by Laudon and Laudon (1993): "a set of interrelated components working together to collect, retrieve, process, store, and disseminate information for the purpose of facilitating planning, control, coordination, and decision making in businesses," and make it time and place independent. Furthermore, although we refer to the Internet as an independent technology in Figure 5.1, it also provides the underlying basis for all other technologies listed there. This is so because the Internet provides the underlying glue for communication. As late Prof. Kazamasky (2003) called it, the Internet has evolved into a "mind map," providing the ideal conduit for communications between disparate "parts" such as individuals, organizations and governments. And being a network of computers without any central control or organization, the Internet has provided unique opportunities as well as challenges in terms of information processing as well as communications. The resulting Global Information System (GIS) comes close to the definition of Palvia et al.'s, (1992) definition of a GIS as "a computerized system which supports the business strategy of a multinational organization and deals with components of the international market as a single market and not as individual markets." Let us have a brief look at each of these technologies before delving deeper into them:

- *Internet technology* – This may be described as a suite of technologies that make use of a network of computers connected to each other using a common transfer protocol and without any centralized control. This technology has been rapidly evolving and adapting to the modern business environment. Organizations need to consider the diverse aspects of the Internet when they apply it to the process of GET. Some of these aspects are identified as: the system architecture, software and applications, database and connectivity, hardware, security and telecommunications. Occasionally, these aspects of the Internet technology are also referred to as a "platform" on which global information systems can be developed and deployed.

- *Extranet and Intranet* – This provides mechanisms for a range of communication of information within a well defined boundary, particularly an organization. Thus, when using the Intranet, it is necessary for organizations to identify the boundary and scope of the usage of this communication mechanism in the early stages of global information systems development. Extranet extends the scope of the Intranet to include controlled access of the organization's data, to applications belonging to authorized external organizations. As we shall see later, this provides uniquely interesting opportunities in the process of GET.

- *Middleware technology* – With an evolving global environment, computer systems no longer consist of a single large computer servicing an organization's information processing needs. Instead, multiple computers interconnected by networks are used to manage and process information. These various computers are brought together or "gelled" by means of middleware technologies. Middleware also provides for uniform interfaces between disparate technologies/applications.

- *Web Services (WS)* – Since Web services provide a standardized way by which applications can communicate across networks, regardless of their size or the computing platform on which they are executing at either ends of the interaction. This results in a genuine independence for businesses interacting and collaborating with each other. Web services (WS) herald a new paradigm in the way businesses transform themselves into global businesses, as WS facilitate direct application-to-application interactions (this is the definition of middleware), thus obviating the need to interact through persons. (Web services can be called the next iteration/implementation of middleware.)

- *Groupware technology* –This is technology designed to facilitate the work of groups. This technology can be applied to communicate, cooperate, coordinate, solve problems, compete, or negotiate. In the information technology context, groupware refers to a specific class of technologies relying on modern computer networks, such as e-mail, calendar and scheduling, newsgroups, or videophones.

- *IT Architecture* – This specifies all business functions covered in a Global Information System (GIS) and defines important concepts and relationships among the components (Treese & Stewart, 1998). The IT architecture is needed for the development of a Global Information System to facilitate and ensure flexibility in GET. The IT architecture encompasses functional, network, software and security architectures. Functional architecture is the architecture designed from the business viewpoint of Information Systems. It is quite different from network architecture and software architecture in terms of their distinct objectives, features, and level of information systems development cycle. Functional architecture plays a significant role in the development of Global Information Systems. It needs to be flexible enough to provide the full operation of Global Information Systems within and across organizations.

- *Global Business* – This is the new globalized business resulting from the effect of the enabling technologies. This is the same business we envisioned in Chapter I. It is shown here in Figure 5.1 as the result of the enabling technologies.

- *Global Management* – This is the management dealing with the effects of the enabling technologies. Obviously, the principles and practices of "standard management" undergo fundamental changes when it comes to globalized e-businesses. For example, principles of control, authority (and its distribution), management of deliverables across geo-political boundaries and application of legal and tax principles all undergo a change in a global environment resulting from enabling technologies.

Internet Technology Relevant to GET

Brief Historical Perspective

Conceived first by the Advanced Research Projects Agency (ARPA) of the U.S. government in 1969, and first known as the ARPANET, the Internet was put together with the aim of enabling research computers to communicate with each other - initially in the domain of educational and non-profit organizations. Soon after, in the 1970s, the first e-mail program was created and the TCP/IP protocol was developed to allow diverse computer networks to interconnect and communicate with each other. Ethernet was also developed in this period, which allowed coaxial cable to carry fast traveling data between computers. In the early 1980s, the University of Wisconsin created the Domain Name System (DNS), which allowed packets to be directed to a domain name where it would be translated by the server database into the corresponding IP number. Thus, the Internet users could access other servers by keying domain names rather than a 12-digit IP address. The value of this ability to identify domain names rather than IP addresses paved the way for business usage of the Internet, and can be seen even today in the ease with which people are able to access regular simple Web sites and utility services by merely using the associated domain names. The Internet usage led to a rapid need for, and increase in, connectivity. In 1985, the National Science Foundation (NSF) began deploying the new T1 backbone lines (1.544Mbps). In 1991, the World Wide Web (WWW) was released by the Corporation for Research and Educational Networking (CREN) and an year later, as reported by Gromov (1995), the National Science Foundation Network (NSFNET) upgraded the backbone to T3 (44.736Mbps). 1995 saw the business world propelled into a "domain name-based" business, and we started entering the "dot com" era: traffic on the Internet grew at an exponential rate and the online services market exploded with businesses vying with each other to get a foothold in the WWW market. During this era, and even today, most Internet traffic is carried by backbones of independent ISPs (e.g., Telstra, Optus, AT&T and UUnet). Currently, the Internet is gearing up for the next "wave" of Nano-technologies and Quantum computing (for discussion on these technologies, see Wilson et al., 2003). This is resulting in initiatives like the Internet Society's vision of a new TCP/IP standard/implementation that would have billions of addresses, rather than the limited 12 digits of an IP address today.

Internet Features Relevant to Global Business

Although the Internet started from the academic domain, as the connectivity and its reliability improved, businesses rapidly spurred forward and capitalized on it. Today, it is a worldwide system of computer networks providing a public, cooperative and self-sustaining facility, providing accessibility to millions of people, businesses and governments, resulting in a rapidly changing fabric of society and culture at large. The "wave" of the communication age enabled by the Internet has been massive enough to force businesses and governments to incorporate the Internet as part of their business and technology strategies. This has resulted in the businesses and governments undertaking a comprehensive set of strategic decisions based on content management, database applications, Web programming, and a range of Internet access technologies. The Internet promised enormous potential for a global business and that potential is being put to good use by many businesses that understand the ability of the Internet to facilitate this globalization. Following are some of the features that make the Internet the technology for globalization:

*   *Global reach* - The Internet reaches nearly everywhere in the world. Most developed and even developing countries provide abundant coverage in terms of Internet connectivity. With continuing and drastic reductions in hardware costs, the availability of computers and equivalent gadgets to enable access to the Internet is also becoming commonplace. Interestingly, countries and regions without appropriate telecommunications technology are finding support from the developed nations to improve their Internet access, especially as the need of the latter to have access to the developing regions is itself increasing. Thus, through vested

interests, or otherwise, the Internet is now covering most parts of the world.

- *Large user population base* – Based on "Nielsen NetRatings Internet users tracking service," in February 2002, the worldwide Internet Population was around 445.9 million. This includes small businesses and home users, perhaps the fastest growing Internet user sectors. As per the Australian Bureau of Statistics (2002) in Australia, 1.2 million small businesses used the Internet to find information and deal with customers during 2001. And these numbers are continuously increasing.

- *Accessibility* – It is extremely simple and straightforward to connect to any other computer through the Internet. Once connected to the Internet, users can access, share and exchange information between other computers independent of their location. This has opened up the possibility of applying this technology in businesses and organizations with specific and special needs (e.g., hospitals, nursing homes, schools, airports).

- *Availability* – Components required to access the Internet (such as hardware, software, communication links, manuals and help) are broadly available in all later models of personal computers. Usually the Internet browser and connection software are included in all new personal computers and most new gadgets such as Pocket PCs and mobile phones. This has facilitated the proliferation of "Internet Cafes" that have a valuable role to play in developing nations where people without computer ownership are also able to communicate globally.

- *Ease of use* – The installation of software packages and the setup of the initial connections are themselves becoming easier and "out of the box." With small-time attempts requiring no specific computing knowledge, users are able to install and connect their computers to the Internet. Furthermore, embedded instructions (install wizards) are usually available to guide users through the installation and setup. Once the user is connected to the Internet, browsing is a convenient method of experiencing the Internet.

- *Low costs* - Sending and obtaining information through the Internet is extremely economical in comparison with telephone calls and the fax transmission of business documents, and even more so when it comes to communication with the other side of the world. The ubiquitous e-mails have not only reduced transmission costs, but have also cut down on paper usage. Same is the case with electronic versions of most newspapers. And features such as "net-to-phone" and "voice over IP" are increasing in popularity in a way that is challenging the traditional telephone companies.

- *Valuable and timely Information* – Users have opportunities to select and obtain fruitful information and knowledge published on the Internet by government organizations, educational institutions, and many others. This is very helpful in reducing the bureaucracy involved in getting simple information – especially from councils and government organizations.

- *Interactivity* – Users are encouraged to communicate with Web sites interactively. For example, users may wish to request information, post comments, obtain feedback, respond to other users' queries and so forth. Thus, users are in full control and enjoy this interactivity much more. As a result, organizations owning these Web sites have developed better relationships with customers (the Internet users).

- *Level Playing field* – The size of a business is less important than the value the business offers. Therefore, having a physical office space is not mandatory to conduct world wide business on the Internet.

Internet Issues Related to Global Business

In order to fully utilize the above Internet benefits, organizations need to be aware of several issues that would detract from the Internet's usefulness and pose disadvantages to the businesses. We discuss them here with the aim of considering them and assuaging their impact during the process of globalization.

- *Reliability of Information and Connectivity* – Information found on the Internet is as reliable as information anywhere. However, the authenticity of the information depends on the credibility of the source or the organization providing that information. However, because the nature of the Internet enables anyone to publish whatever they please and the parties are not always available to validate it, much of the material tends be quite subjective and sometimes downright wrong. Also, an unbroken connection for the duration of a transaction is important in banking and financial transactions, for example, and lack of such reliable connectivity can lead to loss of business confidence.

- *Copyright* – Once an organization puts information onto the Internet, it is available across the world. The information could include the organizations general background in text, pictures, graphics or drawings of product specifications, and all the design ideas and constructs which go with them. Since the material is being accessed in physically far away lands, the problems related to violation of copyright are greatly increased. Furthermore, due to different rules and regulations governing such violations in different countries, the chances of justice being applied in case of infringements is reduced.

- *Computer viruses* – These pose one of the major threats to sustainability of business activities using the Internet. While usually spread through the opening of infected e-mails, computer viruses also continue to proliferate through transfer of files or any other exchange of information from the Internet to local computers and servers. For example, opening a Web page or a file from an FTP site can easily cause a virus to be downloaded onto the local computer. Therefore, it is better to download files from reputable FTP servers, and to use virus-checking software regularly in any GIS applications.

- *Standards* – This is for interoperability. This becomes significant when the globalization process is based on Web services, wherein the ability to publish, locate and consume services depends heavily on standards. Operating systems and security also provide challenges in terms of standardization because different operating systems create problems in terms of interchanging of data and information.

- *Security* – This is one of the major issues that continues to raise concerns with all those involved with the Internet. There is almost an uncountable number of ways that an organization's e-business Web site could be attacked by hackers, crackers and disgruntled insiders. Serious damage could be caused when the e-business Web site is connected with the organization's internal Information Systems.

- *Legal issues* – Although the Internet makes it easier, technologically, for organizations to expand or interact with other organizations, that is not always the case legally. It is essential to consider the implications of going global in terms of "local" legal rules and regulations.

- *Social issues* – Consideration of the differences in the social fabric of the country or region where the organization is expanding globally can be crucial to its success. The Internet provides a challenge even in terms of the ubiquitous e-mail exchanges when it comes to language, color selection, symbols and their meanings, to mention a few.

Internet Accessibility Options

Deciding on the method of Internet access is the initial point for organizations to put their e-business operations into implementation. The appropriate access method for organizations undergoing GET depends on two important features: bandwidth required and cost. The available bandwidth depends upon the type of connection device. Generally, the higher the bandwidth the more expensive the connection and access costs. As businesses continue to move to the Internet, high-speed access has become a significant and strategic component of a globalizing business. However, the competing claims of various providers often make it difficult to know which technology is best for the organization. It is worth considering briefly, some of these access methods, and their particular characteristics that are relevant to the type and size of organizations undertaking the GET process.

Dial-Up

A dial-up connection uses a modem through the phone network to connect to the Internet. This is the most popular and inexpensive type of Internet access. Both organizations and individuals are able to use dial-up connections to access the Internet anywhere (at home or office). This type of connectivity is important from the consumer's viewpoint, as large numbers of home users of the Internet still have dial-up capabilities only. This requires an understanding of these types of customers by organizations trying to extend their reach to global markets. Furthermore, such a connection is also important for a small to medium enterprise that is not technologically savvy but aims to interact with other organizations or individuals primarily for information dissemination rather than for conducting transactions. Limited speed is the main concern for organizational users. Typical dial-up connection speeds are 28.8K, 33.6K and 56.6Kbps.

ADSL

ADSL (Asymmetric Digital Subscriber Line) transmits an asymmetric data stream with a higher bandwidth for downloading data than for uploading data. It is oriented towards SOHOs (Small Offices, Home Offices) and Small and Medium Enterprises (SMEs) that need to conduct transactions on the Internet (as opposed to merely providing and gaining information on the Internet) as well as residential users and home office users who need to download large files. ADSL is based on the telephone infrastructure, however, it is not widely available everywhere. The cost of ADSL connection is more expensive than dial-up connection due to the faster transmission speeds. Thus ADSL targets B2C (Business to Consumer) and elementary B2B (Business to Business) markets. Transmission speed varies from 256Kbps to 1.5Mbps for downloads and from 64Kbps to 256Kbps for uploads (Telstra, 2002a).

Cable

Cable connections enable computers to connect to the Internet through cable modems and a corresponding coaxial cable. Often the same coaxial line is used for Internet connectivity that carries the cable TV service. A cable Internet connection typically uses the bandwidth provided by an unused television channel. The cost of a cable connection is more or less the same as ADSL, however it is not as widely available as the ADSL, especially in some rural areas where cable infrastructure is considered to be an unfeasible investment. The main customer domain is the individual home user who has an existing cable TV facility. For this reason, it is mainly focused on the B2C market with a customer profile similar to the one discussed in the Dial-up section. The speed varies depending on how many subscribers are signed up in a particular area. The maximum is about 30Mbps, but more typical speeds are less than those of a 10Mbps Ethernet LAN (Telstra, 2002b).

Satellite

Satellite Internet access is ideal for rural Internet users who require broadband access. It is also an ideal mechanism to *transition* businesses in developing nations that do not yet have physical connectivity and where providing it is not possible due to the terrain and/or costs. Satellite connections can be used to access the Internet virtually anywhere. For example, a mining company situated in Coober Pedy[1] (an opal mining town in South Australia) requires a satellite connection to facilitate daily mining data transmission to its head office through the company's Web site and to access the company's Internet-based information systems. Satellite Internet does not use telephone lines or cable systems, but instead uses a satellite dish for two-way (upload and download) data communications. Upload speed is about one-tenth of the 500 kbps download speed. Two-way satellite Internet uses Internet Protocol (IP) multicasting technology, which means that up to 5,000 channels of communication can simultaneously be served by a single satellite.

ISDN

ISDN (Integrated Service Digital Network) was designed for digital data and voice transmission. ISDN can have two 64Kbps channels, one for voice and one for data. The two channels can be combined to provide up to 128Mbps. This form of connectivity is expensive but at the same time obviates the limitations of speed, security and reliability that result from other forms of connectivity discussed earlier. Therefore, this is ideal connectivity for globalizing enterprises that are medium to large in size, turnover and physical spread. ISDN provides a stable and continuous connection to organizations that rely heavily on data transmission across the Internet. ISDN connection can be categorized as a part of the B2B market facilitators and is ideally suited for not only transactive usage of the Internet but also collaborative usage, as expected with increasing application of Web services.

Fixed-Point Wireless Internet Access

The new millennium has also heralded the age of wireless communication. This form of communication has resulted from a flurry of development in the wireless data communication equipments and hand-held gadgets, operating systems, corresponding end user applications and wireless networking infrastructure. Common hand-held wireless equipment is suddenly fast enough for useful Internet connections, and wireless is emerging as a revolutionary mainstream technology (as against evolving usage) for business Internet access. Wireless Internet Access in today's world, is usually as fast as land-based connections and, occasionally, even faster (see Table 5.1). Therefore, it is worth noting that wireless connectivity does not compromise speed, as it used to in the early days and, as a result, is ideal for mobile commerce markets for organizations of all sizes and scales.

Table 5.1. Internet access methods

Internet Access Method	Available speed (download/upload)	Cost	Main User Domains	Main/Global Internet Market Domains
Dial-up	56Kbps / 33.6Kbps	Lowest	Individual users	B2C
ADSL	256Kbps - 1.5Mbps / 64Kbps - 256Kbps	Medium	Individual users and small & medium-sized organizations	B2C
Cable	384Kbps- 4.096Mbps / 128Kbps - 2.56Mbps	Medium	Individual users	B2C
Satellite	400Kbps / 33.6Kbps	Medium	Any organization	B2B
ISDN	128Kbps/ 128Kbps	Expensive	Medium to large-sized organizations	B2B
Fixed-point wireless	128Kbps - 1.536Mbps / varies	Expensive	Any organization	Mobile commerce; B2C; B2B
T1 & T3	T1: 1.536Mbps T3: 44.736Mbps	Very expensive	Large organizations	B2B

T1 and T3 Leased Line

A leased line (T1 or T3) is a dedicated, point-to-point, digital Internet connection capable of very high data transfer rates with extremely low latency.

Full T1 service provides a 1.544 Mbps bi-directional high-speed connection to an ISP's backbone. A T3 leased line provides a 45 Mbps connection, which is about 30 times faster than a T1 line. Both T1 and T3 are the ideal Internet access connection from large-scale corporate access needs to hosting e-commerce servers or deploying Intranets, Extranets, VPN (Virtual Private Network) and B2B solutions. These are the most expensive of access types among the methods mentioned above.

Comparison of Internet Access Methods

Table 5.1 summarizes the available transmission speeds, costs, main user domains, and main Internet market domains of each Internet access method. This comparison is useful for globalizing organizations, as people responsible for the GET process get a good understanding of the underlying technology that is needed, or technology that exists but needs to be upgraded, to ensure successful transition. Needless to say, the communication mechanisms need to be complimented with corresponding software applications and business processes, which have been discussed in the earlier chapters.

Extranet-Intranet Usage in Global Business

The previous section discussed the Internet technologies and their application to the GET process. In particular, a variety of Internet connections and their basic characteristics were discussed. However, the connectivity offered by the Internet is not used by globalizing businesses always in its basic form. In fact, there are a number of useful variations to this connectivity offered by the Internet. Two of these variations are the Intranet and the Extranet, as discussed here.

Intranet

While the Internet, as we discussed so far, is the open, unlimited access model, it is also possible that a business may want to "fence off" its access over the Internet to a pre-determined set of users, usually internally to its employees. An intranet is a network within an organization that uses Internet technologies to enable users to find, use, and share documents and Web contents (Bickerton et al., 1998). This results in "private connectivity models" within the organization that provides for and uses a collection of Web resources kept within a firewall for an organization's internal use. As is obvious, the Intranet is relatively secure compared to the Internet, and only provides access to known parties.

Intranets have some similarities to Internet-based Web sites, starting out as departmental or corporate e-mail systems and evolving into a broadcast medium for managing internal information, including Web-based documents as well as access to existing systems and data repositories. Intranets use traditional Internet protocols, TCP/IP and HTTP to transfer data. They usually reside behind firewalls, for security, but are not limited by physical location. In some large companies intranets are used as the primary way for employees to obtain and share work-related documents, share knowledge, collaborate on designs and access e-learning facilities. Thus, in summary, the intranet may be said to have two fundamental functions during globalization:

- Provide secure, customized access to relevant, up-to-date information found in internal business transaction systems; and
- Let users act on that information by managing how it flows through process systems.

Extranet

When a dedicated internal network (Intranet) is opened up in a limited way to a set of known external parties, it becomes an Extranet. Thus an extranet can be viewed as part of a company's intranet that is extended to users outside the company. Extranets use the Internet protocol and the public telecommunication system to securely share part of a business's information or operations with suppliers, vendors, partners, customers, or other businesses (Bickerton et al., 1998). Extranets extend the usage boundary of the organization, encompassing external customers, suppliers, vendors and related business partners (Pfaffenberger, 1998). For example, if a car manufacturer can directly tap into the inventory database of a steel manufacturer (and the steel manufacturer has willingly opened up its database to the car manufacturer), then this connectivity would be called an Extranet. In an extranet-based environment, a customer service system faces both inward towards the customer service personnel and management as well as outward towards the customers themselves, who enjoy a similar level of interactivity and security as an internal participant. As the extranet evolves, it extends not only data but also actual transactions to the Internet to conduct electronic commerce. Similarly, it lends itself to internal global organizational integration by sharing internal and external data with processes that span all existing systems.

Ultranet

As the Internet technology continues to evolve and mature, it has lead to a new form of business network model that is worth mentioning here within the context of GET and that is the Ultranet model. Ultranet conquers the barriers of the traditional client/server model and supports multiple remote connections for flexible access to information within and between organizations. Matsumura (1997) has described this as the new emerging network model. The key elements of Ultranet implementation are foreshadowed by the combined usage of the latest technologies including Java, IPv.6 (Internet Protocol version six), SET (Secure Electronic Transaction), OODBMS (Object-Oriented Database Management System), and XML. The concept of IPv.6 is that every connected device would be provided with a unique identity. Thus, it allows people and collections of databases to link through multiple remote servers and/or devices, instead of the traditional client/server model. This increase in the connectivity and flexibility of delivering and receiving information globally seems to be one of the major benefits for organizations adopting the Ultranet model.

Middleware Technologies

While the aforementioned Internet, Extranet and Intranet provide relatively open connectivity, when it comes to dedicated connectivity between multiple processes running on one or more machines that need to interact across networks, it is provided by what is known as middleware. Middleware results in creation and usage of distributed software that exists between the application and the operating system and network services on a system node in the network (Bernstein, 1996). The relevance of middleware to global information systems is immense as it provides the necessary glue that brings together disparate information systems to enable execution of business processes that depend on multiple applications and databases. This glue becomes more important in the global context because information systems in global organizations are usually spread out physically over many machines, operating systems and business domains. Incorporating middleware and groupware[2] in the organization's global information systems enables machines, applications, people and business processes in different parts of an organization to work together.

Technologically, middleware is essentially a number of well-known architectures and infrastructures that support computer applications to work together across networks. CORBA™ (Common Object Request Broker Architecture), Model Driven Architecture (MDA) and Distributed Common Object Model (DCOM) are some of the common examples of the implementation of middleware. In addition, technologies such as dotNET™, Enterprise JavaBeans™, iPlanet™, WebLogic™, and WebSphere™ have also been considered in the area of middleware – as they too provide the necessary "glue" for applications to communicate with each other. However, they are more appropriately discussed under Web Services. Here we discuss the earlier mentioned middleware technologies and standards that enable information systems to be global.

CORBA™

Common Object Request Broker Architecture™ (CORBA™) is the Object Management Group's (OMG) open, vendor-independent architecture and infrastructure that computer applications use to work together over networks (OMG, 2002a). Using the standard protocol IIOP (Internet Inter-ORB Protocol), a CORBA™-based program from any vendor can interoperate with a CORBA-based program from the same or another vendor, on almost any other computer, irrespective of operating system, programming language, and network. This has obvious repercussions to GET, as GET would have situations in which software applications need to interact with each other across platforms.

CORBA™ provides the mechanisms by which objects transparently make requests and receive responses, as defined by OMG's ORB (Object Request Broker). A CORBA ORB provides a wide variety of distributed middleware services. The ORB lets objects discover each other at run time and invoke each other's services. An ORB is much more sophisticated than alternative forms of client/server middleware including traditional Remote Procedure Calls (RPCs), Message-Oriented Middleware (MOM), database stored procedures, and peer-to-peer services. It is the foundation of OMG's Object Management Architecture and, as such, provides the necessary standards for interoperability of applications – a crucial technological aspect of globalization.

DCOM™

Distributed Component Object Model™ (DCOM™) is a Microsoft product that was built from the ground up to allow Interoperability between various Microsoft products operating on the Microsoft range of platforms. Although DCOM™ is a middleware that facilitates communication between distributed applications, it is still only able to facilitate this within the Microsoft domain.

When it came to traversing beyond the Microsoft domain, DCOM™ was not able to provide the necessary glue for application integration.

MDA™

Model Driven Architecture™ (MDA™) is the latest development in standardizing architectural modeling and information systems integration solutions by OMG (Object Management Group, 2002b). The MDA™ defines an approach to IT system specification that separates the specification of system functionality from the specification of the implementation of that functionality on a specific technology platform (OMG, 2000c). The MDA™'s core architecture is based on the existing OMG's modeling standards including UML (Unified Modeling Language), MOF (Meta-Object Facility) and CWM (Common Warehouse Meta-model).

The MDA supports the UML modeling standard, which is the mechanism that integrates and implements technologies such as Java, XML or Web Application Servers such as WebLogic™ and Web Sphere™.

MDA provides the following features to its users:

- Organizations are able to build new MDA™-based applications with the flexibility of choosing the middleware. This provides a platform independent of the applications and allows any future needs to migrate to a different brand/type/need-specific middleware.

- MDA-based applications are inter-operable with other MDA™-based applications internally in the organization as well as inter-connectable with suppliers, customers, and other business partners. This feature enables organizations to establish a consistent architecture in both internal and external operations.

- The function of integration provided by MDA™ is important for the organization's existing information systems that has a large legacy heritage and needs to be integrated with the new global information system architecture. The MDA™ standards facilitate the development of new software applications while preserving the investment in the existing business processes and operations.

- Developers are provided with the ultimate flexibility in code generation from a platform-independent model. The application module reusability and domain-specific model provide organizations with a faster return on investment period and the applications are supported and maintained in a long-term cost-effective cycle.

- Application models are developed, viewed, and manipulated via UML, transmitted via XMI, and stored in MOF repositories, resulting in enhanced quality and interoperability.

Web Services in GET

Evolution of component technologies and distributed computing together with that of the Internet has resulted in the development/identification of a set of technologies that are now referred to as Web services (WS). As compared to distributed computing, where there was a dedicated distribution platform, in Web services, the exchange of information and data is primarily through document-based XML that can be easily exchanged between software applications on a wide variety of platforms (for detailed discussion on comparison of middleware technologies with those of WS, see Chaturvedi and Unhelkar, 2003). This has lead to WS being heralded by many as the next "big thing" in software technologies, and has been considered as a way to capitalize on the existing software assets, accelerate business e-transformations and also reduce costs and improve efficiencies. Web Services may be considered as one of the key elements for a dynamic e-business and m-business. Despite the occasionally reported lull in the adoption of WS by Gartner Research and other firms, there is also an expectation of accelerated growth in the adoption of WS as companies complete their learning stages, overcome their initial reluctance to using Web services, and start to realize the potential of this technology in globalization. With maturing WS, it should be expected that this technology would be used in major globalization processes. These are the reasons why WS is being discussed in detail here.

What are Web Services?

As mentioned earlier, Web services provide the next level in enabling applications to "glue together" by providing an ability to *publish, locate* and *consume* applications. The World Wide Web Consortium (W3C) has the following definition of a Web service:

"A Web service is a software system identified by a Universal Resource Identifier (URI) whose public interfaces and bindings are defined and described using eXtensible Markup Language (XML). Its definition can be discovered by other software systems. These systems may then interact with the Web service in a manner prescribed by its definition, using XML-based messages conveyed by Internet protocols."

Another definition on the W3C Web site states:

"A Web service is a software system designed to support interoperable machine-to-machine interaction over a network. It has an interface described in a machine-processable format (specifically WSDL). Other systems interact with the Web service in a manner prescribed by its description using SOAP messages, typically conveyed using HTTP with an XML serialization in conjunction with other Web-related standards."

The earlier discussion on middleware is reminiscent of the attempts made by the IT community to provide similar interactive frameworks through DCOM, CORBA™ and RMI. While those middleware components promised a lot, they were marred by the lack of "open" technologies. With Web services, though, the promise is of open connectivity. While still struggling with the lack of proper industry wide regulation at the current stage, Web service technologies have far more potential and far more to offer to businesses. This is because, at a very fundamental level, WS enables communication with each other without human intervention (application-to-application communication). At a technical level, this results in Web services enabling integration, collaboration, communication and re-use between applications. Therefore, integrating software applications requires minimal effort – a crucial ingredient in successful expansion and globalization of organizations. We consider some specific advantages of WS in globalization next.

Why Web Services in Globalization?

Web services provide an excellent basis for globalization (Unhelkar, 2003) primarily because of their ability to facilitate business interactions between applications. This opens up the doors to automation of business decisions, business processes and sharing of business tasks. In fact, WS offers an unlimited array of opportunities in the realms of electronic global business. The ability of WS to facilitate technological gluing, and incrementally adding new functions and reusing existing ones, helps businesses in resolving many of their problems in terms of application integrations and data connectivity – challenges that appear more frequently and significantly during the globalization process. As Sanjiv et al. (2003) state:

> *"Web services will ease partner-to-partner interaction, make application integration easier, create new business opportunities, give businesses more and better choices, give enterprises competitive advantages over rivals and improve efficiency in trusted environments."*

Web Services Interactions

Web services promise a number of direct practical uses in the process of globalization. This is because they are based on application-to-application (A2A) patterns that are used by implementers and integrators of software applications. Due to the nature of Web services, their communication abilities are properly utilized by A2A implementations, despite the fact that they may be used by human users through the Internet browsers. The ranges of interactions facilitated by WS include:

- *Between businesses* – e.g., B2B interfaces are directly with partners and suppliers, or via the use of an e-marketplace. However, increasingly through Web services, these B2B interfaces can be more appropriately described as A2A interfaces, wherein applications are able to deal with each other directly, facilitating easier global business processes.

- *Between businesses and end-users* – e.g., client code on user devices, such as Browsers, PDAs, and wireless phones. This will have greater impact on the demands of end users for "comprehensive packaged" services – a "one-stop shop" that is facilitated through Web services. (Will this have an impact on the demands of users or the systems that provide the services OR both? Maybe this increase in use will increase demand

and hence increase in use and so on.... Now, is this to be considered good or bad?)

- *Within a business* – Services that are located only internally within an enterprise, and not exposed to business partners provide great opportunities for globalizing organizations, because they make the task of integrating applications relatively easy. For example, as it globalizes, a large business with extensive legacy applications (typically in COBOL) and data, will require its applications to interact with each other across different platforms and also geographical spaces. This is facilitated by "wrappers" of Web services on top of the existing applications.

Types of Services/Uses of Services

Public vs. Private services – Services which are available for general public use vs. services that are restricted and authorized for use only by specified Service Requesters. A suite of public services, for example, can go a long way in reducing the bureaucratic overloads of government organizations – especially when a large number of interactions with a government organization may be queries.

- *Free and Fee-based services* – Some externally (to an enterprise) exposed Web services are available free for marketing promotion purposes or to facilitate normal business transactions. Others are offered for a fee as a revenue-generating opportunity. Both types of services are likely to add considerable value to organizations undertaking GET in terms of offering as well as consuming services.

- *Information Requests* – Inquiries for information can be made without concern for the underlying database or data model supporting the service. This, as mentioned earlier, is helpful in e-governance, and interaction of globalizing organizations with corresponding bureaucracies.

- *Transactions* – Interactions between applications for the purpose of conducting a transaction can be performed asynchronously or synchronously. These transactions can follow a simple "request and immediate response" pattern, or involve long-running transactions that include complex interactions with multiple systems thereby requiring a longer period of time before a response is provided. Both types of transactions can be used in globalization attempts, as different applications and databases will respond differently to the transactions.

- *ASPs (Application Service Providers)* – Web services could be provided directly from a company's own infrastructure, or though the use of an ASP's infrastructure. Provision of WS through ASPs is important during globalization process of small and medium enterprises, whereas for large organizations, it may not be that relevant. Why? Because the infrastructure needs in terms of upfront costs, maintenance, skills, etc., are not the same.

- *Point-to-Point and Hub approaches* – Like other application interaction modes, Web services can be either point-to-point or through an integration hub (isn't this some extension of middleware/messaging architecture?) that provides for request routing, transformations, or workflow. However, both of these are technology options that are available to the globalizing businesses. It depends on the way in which a business is globalizing and the extent of "clusters" involved in globalization. For a cluster of organizations globalizing simultaneously, a hub approach will be more appropriate.

- *Business process automation* – Business process modeling and corresponding process tools are likely to facilitate industry standardized workflow outputs that can be recorded in a directory and consumed just as other "well-formatted" services are consumed today. For example, while the process of calculating interest based on the interest rate is pretty standardized, the process of evaluating a home loan is more complicated

Figure 5.2. Major technology areas in Web services (based on Unhelkar, 2003)

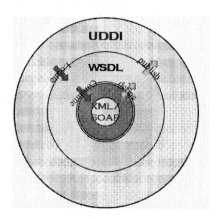

Figure 5.3. XML providing application-to-application glue (based on Unhelkar, 2003)

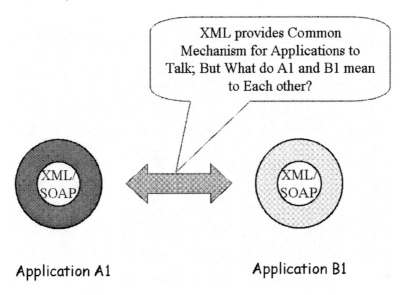

requiring detailed business processes that would encompass multiple organizations in a global environment. In such cases, business process modeling with process tools can provide the opportunity to publish and consume complicated business processes (like the home loan process) electronically through Web services.

Core Elements of Web Services

Having discussed the importance and relevance of the Web service interactions in the context of globalization, let us now consider the core technical elements of Web services, and how they make these interactions feasible. Basically, Web service technologies can be broken down simply into three major and easily recognizable areas, as shown in Figure 5.2.

These technical layers of Web services are: the XML/SOAP protocol and packaging layer; the WSDL definition layer; and the UDDI discovery layer. The XML/SOAP provides the basic means of transferring document-based information and data across the Internet. The WSDL helps in defining the meaning behind the services, and the UDDI layer helps publish and locate

Figure 5.4. Web Service Definition Language (WSDL) facilitates understanding the meaning behind various applications across platforms (based on Unhelkar, 2003)

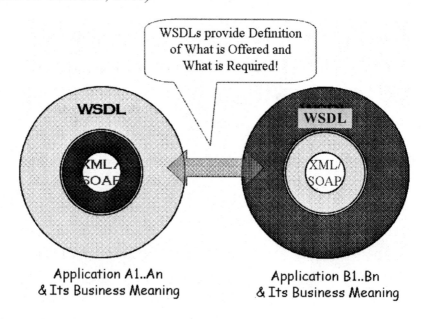

Figure 5.5. UDDI – Universal Description, Discovery, and Integration protocol facilitates application-to-application through open search (based on Unhelkar, 2003)

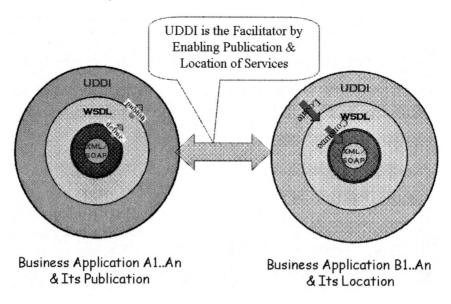

services. These are considered in greater detail in the context of how Application-to-Application interaction is enabled through these technologies.

Relevant XML

XML (eXtensible Markup Language), together with Simple Object Access Protocol (SOAP) provide the "standard" means for Application-to-Application communication. As shown in Figure 5.3, there is communication between applications A1 and B1. This communication is based on messaging technology, leaving the internals of the "other application" usually hidden. This provides unique opportunities in terms of globalization, wherein an application from a business need not worry about the internal implementation of another application from another business, except communicating with it through XML/SOAP.

Web Services Definition Language

Although XML is able to facilitate communication between two applications, it is essential to understand the "meaning" behind these applications. The meaning is defined and described by WSDL – Web Services Definition

Figure 5.6. A Web service meta model

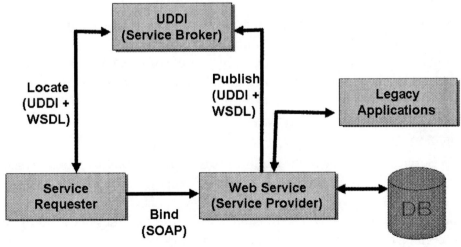

Language, as shown in Figure 5.4. WSDL facilitates the understanding of the meaning, or the business processes underlying each of the applications. Those applications that want to provide services publish their information through WSDL, and it is these WSDLs that are consumed by the user of the service.

Universal Description, Discovery and Integration (UDDI)

While applications interact with the each other using WS in the form of an XML file, and their definitions are put together in WSDL, it is the UDDI that makes the application and its services "known" to the external business world, as also facilitating the ability of users of those services to locate and consume those services. Thus, as shown in Figure 5.5, UDDI provides the ability for business applications to publish and use services, working like an electronic "yellow pages."

Web Services: A Succinct Meta-Model

The technologies of Web services, mentioned in the previous section can be summarized into a meta-model that represents the major elements of Web services and how they relate to each other. Such a meta-model is shown in Figure 5.6. This meta-model is an extension of the technical work done by Monday (2003) that makes it easier to understand the Web services technologies from a business or usage perspective and thereby form the basis of technical understanding of globalization process. Figure 5.6 shows the three major components of Web services and their relationships.

The Service Provider shows the service being offered by a business. This service being offered is a programmatic interface for other applications to interact with the Web service, usually in the form of an XML document. As is obvious, businesses that aspire to operate globally will have to ascertain the types of services they want to offer, handle the business models for such services, and eventually seek ways to publish their services onto a common directory.

The Service Broker shows the facilities provided by a directory provider (such as UDDI). This is also known as the "discovery layer" and is designed to provide a standardized way in which Web services can be centrally registered, located, and published. The existence of a directory (service) is a major discerning factor between what would be a normal Web application and a Web

Figure 5.7. Web services: Putting it all together

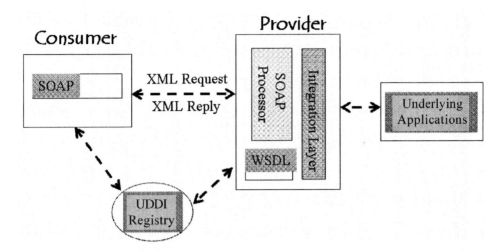

services-based application. The challenges in terms of standardizing the contents and ensuring their availability are not yet fully handled but are issues that impact the way in which a cluster of organizations may decide to globalize their operations.

The Service Requester is the application that is keen to locate and consume the service offered by the provider and made known by the UDDI. Through the use of Web services, service requesters (such as, say, a bank, or a travel agency) have the freedom to put together various offerings as may be available through the directories, to provide their own customer a wide variety of choices. The array of permutations and combinations that service requesters (or clients) can provide through the use of Web services takes the process of globalization to an altogether different paradigm.

Web Services: Architecture for Business

When the aforementioned meta-model is implemented for business, it is represented as in Figure 5.7. This figure shows how the consumer of Web services would first look for the UDDI registry, and having found the provider would send a request to the provider. The WSDL will display what the provider can offer, and the underlying business logic remains hidden from the consumer. Once the consumer's service request is understood by the provider, the service is provided, using the XML/SOAP protocol.

Table 5.2. Elements of the Microsoft® .NET platform

Platform elements	Description
Smart clients and devices	"Smart" client software applications enable PCs and other smart devices to act on XML Web services, allowing anywhere, anytime access to information.
XML Web services	XML Web services are small, reusable component applications that can be connected like building blocks to perform tasks on behalf of users.
.NET servers	The Microsoft .NET server infrastructure is the key to deploying, managing, and orchestrating XML Web services.
Developer tools	By using Microsoft Visual Studio® .NET and the Microsoft .NET Framework as the development tools, developers are able to build, deploy, and run XML Web services.

Web Services: Practical Tools

We have discussed, thus far, the theory and the technologies of WS that facilitate the process of globalization. It is also worth mentioning here some of the practical tools provided by tool vendors that enable creation and implementation of Web services. These tools are themselves a suite of well thought out applications and infrastructures that make it easier to implement Web services. A note of caution, here, though for the enthusiastic implementers of these technologies that merely using one of these tools does not guarantee full utilization of the capabilities of Web services. WS needs to be coupled with the needs of the business to globalize, and the requirement that their applications interact with each other across platforms and machines. Unless Web services are coupled with corresponding business understanding and implementation of the directory services discussed in WS architecture, they are merely going to implement standard applications without realizing their full potential. Some practical tools that are relevant to GET are as follows.

Microsoft® .NET™

Microsoft® .NET is the Microsoft XML Web services platform. XML Web services allow applications to communicate and share data over the Internet, regardless of the operating system, device, or programming language (Microsoft, 2002b). Table 5.2 outlines the four elements (client, services, servers, and tools) of the Microsoft® .NET platform.

The .NET Framework consists of three main parts: the common language runtime, a hierarchical set of unified classes, and a component-based version of Microsoft Active Server Pages known as Microsoft ASP.NET.

The common language runtime is built on top of operating system services. It is responsible for actually executing the application. The runtime supplies many services that help simplify code development and application deployment while improving application reliability.

The unified classes provide a unified, object-oriented, hierarchical, and extensible set of class libraries, or APIs (Application Programming Interfaces), that developers can use from any programming language.

ASP.NET is a set of classes within the unified class library. ASP.NET provides a Web application model in the form of a set of controls and infrastructure that make it simple to build Web applications.

Microsoft® also introduces an object-oriented programming language called "C#" (pronounced "C sharp"). C# is a modern, object-oriented language that enables programmers to quickly build a wide range of applications for the Microsoft .NET platform (Microsoft, 2002a). C# is designed to architect a wide range of components from high-level business objects to system-level applications. These components can be converted into XML for deployment on any platforms.

As the Microsoft® .NET enables software applications to work together among and between organizations, global information sharing and exchanging tasks are easier to control and manage. This is extremely relevant to GET, as it creates greater opportunities to connect with suppliers, customers, and consumers. Also, the ability of employees to access and provide information from anywhere using a smart device, is a major asset of this WS technology during GET.

Corporate Web sites can be seen as one of the important elements for organizations pursuing globalization. The Microsoft® .NET facilitates the ability of Web sites to interact with one another as well as with existing systems and applications.

XML Web services present the opportunity to bridge information and applications written in different programming languages and residing on differing platforms. In this manner, applications from departments in a New York office and a Sydney office can share information.

The Microsoft® .NET allows dispersed employees to work together on a single project. It enhances the way of exchanging information, improves communications with customers, and provides the flexibility of accessing information without having to completely synchronize every user's different IT tools.

The Microsoft® .NET provides a real-time collaboration environment that helps organizations address any operational issues in real-time, anytime, and from anywhere. This results in faster problem resolution and improved capture of distributed enterprise knowledge, leading to shorter development cycles, accelerated time-to-market, higher product quality, and lower development and production costs.

The improvement of development times on the global information system applications is because the .NET Framework provides a single development platform and eliminates the integration and maintenance issues.

Enterprise JavaBeans™

The Enterprise JavaBeans, from SUN, architecture is component architecture for the development and deployment of component-based distributed business applications. Applications written in the Enterprise JavaBeans architecture are scalable, transactional, and multi-user securable. These applications may be written once, and then deployed on any server platform that supports the Enterprise JavaBeans specification (Sun, 2002a).

The main benefits of Enterprise JavaBeans™ over global information systems are:

- It provides the standard for developing distributed business application components in global information systems under the Java™ programming environment.

- It supports multi-vendor components to be combined into applications. For example, cross-border development teams could apply different tools in building application components, and employ the Enterprise JavaBean architecture to integrate the built components into the applications that form parts of the global information systems.

- It provides the ability to distribute the developed components in multiple platforms without the processes of rewriting and recompiling the programming sources.

iPlanet™

iPlanet™ E-Commerce Solutions, a Sun-Netscape Alliance, are built using the extensible open standards of the Sun™ Open Net Environment (Sun ONE)(Sun,

2002b). It aims to provide the interoperability and reusability as the foundation of Web applications and services.

In the global business environment, most organizations began using portals to aggregate enterprise applications into a single interface. Organizations realized that dynamic, personalized Web content delivery is essential to achieve superior portal efficiency, workflow, and usability. iPlanet™ Integration Services are suitable to be applied in the global information systems for complex enterprise application integration (EAI) and secure business-to-business (B2B) integration.

The key features of iPlant™ Integration services are:

- Providing a method for implementing business strategic alliances and partnerships by integrating key Web service standards, described earlier, such as XML, SOAP, WSDL and UDDI.
- Assisting organizations in optimizing information systems development time, business process management, resource aggregation, and partnering opportunities.
- Providing the ability to update the organization's business practices without changing the fundamental technology architecture.

WebLogic™

WebLogic™ is a server application developed by BEA Systems, Inc. (2002), an application infrastructure software company. It is a platform for developing and deploying multi-tier distributed enterprise applications. WebLogic Server centralizes application services such as Web server functionality, business components, and access to backend enterprise systems.

WebLogic™ Server provides essential features for developing and deploying mission-critical e-business applications across distributed, heterogeneous computing environments. These features are:

- Standardization – supports comprehensive Enterprise Java to ease implementation and deployment of application components.
- Rich client options – supports Web browsers and other clients that use HTTP, Java clients that use RMI (Remote Method Invocation) or IIOP

(Internet Inter-ORB Protocol), and mobile devices that use WAP (Wireless Access Protocol).

- Enterprise e-business scalability – critical resources are used efficiently and high availability is ensured through the use of Enterprise JavaBean business components and mechanisms such as WebLogic Server clustering for dynamic Web pages, backend resource pooling, and connection sharing.

- Robust administration – offers a Web-based Administration Console for configuring and monitoring WebLogic Server services.

- Internet payment security readiness – provides Secure Sockets Layer (SSL) support for encrypting data transmitted across WebLogic Server, clients, and other servers.

- Maximum development and deployment flexibility – provides tight integration with and support for leading databases, development tools, and other environments.

- WebLogic Server operates as the middle tier of a multi-tier architecture. A multi-tier architecture determines where the software components that make up a computing system are executed in relation to each other and to the hardware, network, and users.

WebSphere®

In a global organization, daily business transactions flow and are exchanged across dispersed locations. Using the Web as the platform to carry out business transactions appears to be the most efficient and economic channel. However, without the implementation of an appropriate middleware, the internal core business processes cannot be linked with the front-end Web-based operations and further enhance the organization's information flows. WebSphere® (IBM, 2002a) could be considered as the appropriate software to support these requirements. WebSphere® is IBM's brand of Internet infrastructure software or middleware. It enables organizations to develop, deploy and integrate new e-business applications with their existing back office applications. At the same time, WebSphere® supports business applications from simple Web publishing through to enterprise-scale transaction processing.

WebSphere® enables organizations to advance their e-business strategy in three functional areas:

- Provides access to information across a spectrum of users, devices, and customization options.

- Integrates and automates business processes including supply chain management and the integration of existing processes with the Web.

- Builds, connects, and manages applications.

Groupware Technologies

In addition to the previous detailed discussion on Web services, it is also important to discuss another suite of technologies that directly facilitate human communications within and outside teams and that are crucial to successful GET. These technologies are called "Groupware" technologies that appropriately facilitate human communications and control of information flows as an important ingredient of dispersed teams and organizations – typically during globalization process. While reengineering business processes and organizational restructuring are the main trends for modern enterprises towards increasing productivity (Coleman, 1995), when these are coupled with globalization, there is an acute need to use technology itself to facilitate communication. Thus, groupware helps organizations in their attempts to expand and at the same time reduce costs (such as sales, labor and communications costs), increase quality, provide better customer services by having greater employee autonomy, flexibility and responsiveness in order to survive in the global competitive edge. Accordingly, efficient human and information communications seem to be the essential foundation to achieve these objectives. Groupware technology en-

Figure 5.8. Four options in groupware usage

	Same time "synchronous"	Different time "asynchronous"
Same Place	- voting - presentation support	- shared computers
Different Place	- videophones - chat	- e-mail - workflow

ables people and teams, which are physically separate, to work together effectively. As compared with middleware, discussed earlier in this chapter wherein disparate information systems and applications are brought together, and Web services, which focus on bringing applications and software together, groupware brings people together. And this ability of groupware to facilitate people interactions is not limited to an organization or a country, but is literally a bridge between differing people with different values and cultures. Thus, groupware brings functionality into full play in the global information systems where dispersed employees are able to collaborate and accomplish corporate assignments.

Groupware technologies are typically categorized along two key dimensions (Bock and Marca, 1995), as shown in Figure 5.8.

Users of the groupware are working together at the same time ("real-time" or "synchronous" groupware) or different times ("asynchronous" groupware), and users are working together in the same place ("face-to-face") or in different places ("distance").

A number of typical groupware applications that fall within the above categories and that are important within the GET context are e-mail, newsgroups/mailing lists, workflow systems, group calendars, shared whiteboards, and decision support systems. Let us consider some of the practical groupware applications that help in the globalization process.

Lotus Notes®

Lotus Notes® is a well-known groupware developed by Lotus Corporation and owned by IBM (2002b). It is a very popular groupware application for workgroups. Basically, Lotus Notes® provides group communications for creation and access of document-oriented information over LANs (Local Area Networks), WANs (Wide Area Networks), and dial-up connections. It also has capabilities to combine documents, e-mails, and group calendars and conferences. Lotus Notes® contains one or more Notes servers that are connected to the Notes clients over the organization's network.

Key features of Lotus Notes® are:

- It integrates organizational information sources including e-mail, calendar, address book, action list, the Web site and e-business applications, and allows users to access them seamlessly online or off-line.

- It offers a single, integrated in-box for Notes mail and Internet mail, from Internet Service Providers (ISPs).

- Integrated with Lotus Sametime, it allows users to see who is online, send instant messages and chat in real-time.

- The group calendar function allows users in the workgroup or project team with the appropriate access permission to see all members' schedules.

- It fully supports X.509 certificates[3] (public-key certificates) and S/MIME[4] (Secure / Multipurpose Internet Mail Extensions) that enable its users to send and receive signed and/or encrypted messages via the Internet.

Microsoft® Exchange Server

Another popular groupware application is Microsoft® Exchange Server (2002c). Exchange Server is a messaging platform that enables a range of solutions for the free exchange of e-mail, voice mail, streaming video, documents, and Web content, video-conferencing, instant messaging, and chat sessions.

Core features of Exchange Server include:

- It offers integrated management of the organization's networking and messaging infrastructure.

- It supports instant messaging to overcome barriers of time, distance and architectures, encapsulated designs, reuse considerations in design, programming through interfaces (e.g., Application Programming Interfaces - APIs).

- It incorporates the latest digital technologies such as instant messaging and real-time conferencing in a communication platform for all organization users.

- It delivers built-in services such as calendaring, contact and task management, discussion groups, and document-centric workflow as well as support for Web-standard protocols, including XML and HTTP (Hypertext Transfer Protocol).

Global IT Architecture

Having discussed so far in detail the Internet technologies, and the gluing mechanisms of Middleware, Groupware and Web services, we now discuss the important technical issue of Information Technology architecture. It is important to be aware of the IT architectural issues in global enterprise transitions, as they have an impact on not only the technological capabilities but also business capabilities of the globalizing business. The IT architecture provides the mainstay for applications, and enables putting together different systems, platforms, applications and networks. Architecture helps in both Integration and Transition aspects of business applications and therefore is discussed as an interwoven part of the GET. The specific technical issues that architecture considers with respect to software systems are as follows:

- *Scalability* – Software systems need to grow and expand with the corresponding growth in the globalizing business. This requires that the provisions for this growth are placed in the system right at the onset – a job of architecture. Growth issues, that require the system to be scalable, are in terms of expansion of services offered, growth in the number of users, increase in the volume of their transaction values, increased demand for newer services and so on.

- *Adaptability* – The technology must enable the organization to upgrade and integrate its enterprise resources and customer relationship management systems. The adaptability of the IT services within the organization is what will allow it to survive sudden changes in the market and with the competition. Some of the mechanisms that allow the core business systems to be adaptable and agile are component-based architectures, encapsulated designs, reuse considerations in design, programming through interfaces (e.g., Application Programming Interfaces – APIs).

- *Availability* – The systems must be capable of providing a 24 x 7 x 365 service to customers, which is essential to serve users on the global platform. The organization has to be aware that its new e-customers will be online on a 24 x 7 x 365 basis, which means that there will be customers connected at any time anywhere in the world to locate and use various e-services. The expectations and interests of users in the content and services being offered will vary depending on the changing needs of the users as well as the environment in which they operate.

Table 5.3. Significance of functional, network, software and security architectures

	Functional architecture	Network architecture	Software architecture	Security architecture
Objectives	Business views of information systems	Technical communication views of information systems	Technical component views of information systems	Ensuring business confidence in global information systems
Features	Identifying and understanding roles of potential users, and decomposition of business processes into smaller functional units	Based on the seven layers of the OSI model	Variety of architectural styles in the categories of dataflow systems, call-and-return systems, independent components, virtual machines, and data-centered systems	Based on global security protocols and standards
Level/stages	Early analysis stage	Early design stage	Design stage	Early design stage

- *Compatibility* – Technologies used must be "highly" compatible with competitors and potential partners, as well as being in line with the development of newer technologies. For example, XML and MQ-Message are some of the increasingly popular information sharing mechanisms in the information industry. Attention must be continuously paid to emerging and published XML standards.

- *Reliability* – Systems must be reliable and available at all times. Business Continuity and Disaster Recover procedures and systems need to be tested and in place as a part of proper architectural work.

- *Maintainability* – All systems require some level of maintenance but the production systems maintenance and testing are carefully planned during less disruptive periods like Easter and Christmas.

Comparison of Architectures

Although functional, network, software and security architectures are all built for information systems, they are quite different in their features and objectives as well as the level and stage (of development, application, implementation, relevance, etc.) of information systems development. The following table (Table 5.2) summarizes these architectures in terms of objectives, features, and relevant stages in the information systems development cycle.

Functional Architecture

Functional architecture deals with the architecture of the information system as viewed by the business. It deals with understanding, modeling and improving on the way information is captured, analyzed and presented to the users. As functional architecture depends on the nature of the business, different types of businesses would have different architectures. For example, an architecture developed for a department store system might be very different from that for a travel and tours system.

As mentioned in the previous section, functional architecture is considered as an abstract view of the organization in terms of business processes. It could be interpreted as the senior executive's vision of the business in the context of information systems. This helps distinguish the functional architecture from other architectures such as the network architecture and software architecture.

It is very important to have a general functional architecture in global information systems. The reason is that as the business refines and evolves its strategic vision and business operations, the information systems will need to evolve as well. This is even critical during the global transition process.

The core idea of the functional architecture is to develop appropriate and flexible global information systems that can be unreservedly operated within and across the organization. To do this, the organization must address issues related to the global transition process and identify possible solutions. In some cases, these issues are considered explicitly during the development phase. In other cases, these issues and their solutions are reflected in assumptions about various components in the architecture.

The approach of developing a successful architecture involves two important ingredients: understanding of roles and decomposition of functions (Treese & Stewart, 1998).

Understanding of Roles

Understanding various roles and users for the organization's information systems helps the organization to ensure the developed information systems will meet the objectives of the business visions and facilitate users to accomplish daily business activities. It is more crucial in the global business environment than where organizations operate only locally. In global information systems, business units are dispersed everywhere over the world and users are from different backgrounds, cultures, and have quite distinct social expectations. In order to make sure each user carries out business tasks smoothly, understanding the potential roles of users is suggested as the essential primary stage in the development of global information systems.

Decomposition of Functions

The second important part of functional architecture is to decompose business processes into smaller functional units. In global information systems development, a single business process may be operated through multiple business units (such as subsidiaries or branches). Applying the functional decomposition method to partition business processes into functional units and identifying the interface/interaction between functional units could reduce the complexity and confusion in the system architecture design phase. Moreover, it helps the organization to identify any unnecessary functions that could be eliminated or reengineered as well as enhancing certain valuable functions.

Network Architecture

Network architecture deals with the technical communication components of the information systems. It provides the architecture of communications between computers. The two essential components of the network architecture are firstly compatible hardware, and secondly, compatible software. By analogy to the telephone system, for two households to communicate, they both must use telephone receivers that operate on the same electrical principles, connected to the same cabling system (hardware) and they both must use the same language when speaking (software).

The design of any network architecture is often based upon the OSI (Open Systems Interconnect) seven-layer network model (Day & Zimmermann, 1983) that was codified by the International Standards Organization.

The OSI seven layers are briefly outlined as follows:

- Physical – cable or media standards.
- Data Link – format of data on the network and how it flows.
- Network – provide routing and related functions that enable multiple physical network segments to be combined into an "Internetwork."

- Transport – provide reliable process-to-process communication.

- Session – the concept of tying to bring multiple transport streams into a single "session."

- Presentation - issues of data format conversion, compression, encryption, and so on.

- Application – the actual implementation of software applications by users.

Software Architecture

Software architecture involves the description of components from which systems are built, interactions among those components, patterns that guide their composition, and constraints on these patterns (Shaw & Garlan, 1996). Ideally, each component is defined and designed independently, thus the component can be reused within different contexts.

The characteristics of software architecture are:

- It is at a high-enough level of abstraction that the system can be viewed as a whole.

- The structure must support the functionality required of the system. Therefore, the dynamic behavior of the system must be taken into account when designing the architecture.

- The architecture must conform to the system qualities (also known as non-functional requirements). These quality requirements include the software performance, security and reliability requirements associated with current functionality, as well as flexibility or extensibility requirements associated with accommodating future functionality at a reasonable cost to change. Some of these may conflict and require alternatives, but it is essentially part of the software architecture design.

- At the software architectural design level, all implementation details are hidden.

- A variety of architectural styles (patterns) exist that can be utilized to analyze, model and construct a system. Each style has capabilities that are suitable for use in their specific areas. These range from pipe-and-filter descriptions to others that allow for more complex interactions and reuse.

Security Infrastructure

Access Security

All good security infrastructures must incorporate acceptable use of networks and computers in the form of policies. These policies must be disseminated and enforced. For instance, password policy will determine how passwords are created, how often they are reviewed and how frequently they should be changed. This is especially important within the context of GIS, as the users of such systems are unknown, and may not always be the employees or known customers. The level of access is also important as different user levels will require different facilities and access to the GIS. It is important that in all globalizing organizations, policy on e-mail access and use is instituted and made known.

Firewalls and Security

The purpose of a firewall is to protect the organization's internal network from outside observation and intruders. It provides protection from unauthorized intrusions and allows authorized external systems/users access to the appropriate internal systems. Firewalls provide the ability to set up rules and filters to examine any information that is sent across the boundaries of the organization with the external world.

In addition to a firewall that regulates the connectivity to external sources (mainly from authorized external sources to internal systems), an e-mail scanning software is essential to eliminate the possibility of suspicious/malicious attachments from being received and compromising the security of the organization from the inside.

A router provides another level of security in that it allows for private addressing within an organization and allows for one external IP address to be used to communicate with the wider Internet. This protects inside addresses from outside access (Kalakota & Whinston, 1997).

Access and Authorization

Authentication is the process by which access to resources is controlled. It is essential to be able to identify users. The process might involve the various methods from valid user name and password combinations to token-based technologies and digital certificates. The security solution should define and control exactly which resources users are allowed to use. Global organizations need to ensure that an appropriate security infrastructure is in place.

Security is enhanced when the entire transaction travels under the protection of public-key encryption, with the digital certificate verifying the purchaser's identity, the digital wallet hiding the card data, and the encryption rendering the transaction difficult to hack (Penny & Randall, 2002).

Methodologies in Software

While we are discussing technologies, it is worth mentioning that in application of all technologies(especially information and communication technologies), the software methodologies should always be considered. Software methodologies (or processes) have been discussed in detail by Unhelkar (2003). Due consideration to the methodological aspects of software development and application is essential to enable the software aspect of the GET process to have consistency and quality. This results in a high level of confidence in approaching software development, especially if a part of the software development has to be outsourced (a common scenario in many software development projects). In addition to the focused software development methodologies, it is also essential to integrate these methodologies with the project management aspects of software development. There are many significant aspects of project management that are helpful in successful management of global information systems implementations, as would be expected in a GET process. As a reminder, some of the significant aspects of managing software projects with methodologies include the following:

Scope definition, Requirements engineering, Scalable architecture, Client/ User experience, Project and resource management, Change management and project control, Security, Quality assurance, Change Control, Risk management, Documentation, and Training and support.

Technology Future in GIS

Before concluding on technologies, it is also worth mentioning the impact some of the newer technologies are having on global information systems (GIS) as applied Agents are computer programs that accomplish activities *without direct human interaction.* For example, hiding details, monitoring, training, tasking can be some activities that can be achieved by sending a program across the computer network to another node or workstation, wherein it will perform tasks as required. Agents need good, reliable knowledge base and ability to communicate with other Programs. Some examples of practical agents in global information systems include:

PersonaLogic (constraint algorithm to retrieve ordered sets), Firefly (auto collaborative filters to rate and recommend products), BargainFinder & Jango (performance and price comparisons); Help in Bidding and Negotiations.

Summary

In this chapter, we discussed the significance of technology in the global enterprise transition process. The technologies of Web services were discussed in detail as the next major wave after the middleware technologies, which would enable A-to-A interaction. The specific tools that help in globalization were also mentioned. This completes our understanding of the globalization process. We now look at a case study in the last chapter of this book, in which these discussions so far are applied.

References

Adam, Dogramaci, Gangopadhyay & Yesha. (1999). *Electronic commerce: Technical, business and legal issues.* New York: Prentice-Hall.

Australian Bureau of Statistics. (2002). *Information technology Australia.* Australian Bureau of Statistics Catalogues.

BEA. (2002). e-docs.bea.com. BEA Systems Inc. Retrieved March22, 2002 from the World Wide Web at: *http://edocs.bea.com*

Bernstein, P.A. (1996). Middleware: A model for distributed services. *Communications of the ACM, 39*(2), 86-97.

Bickerton, P., Bickerton, M. & Siimpson-Holley, K. (1998). *Cyberstrategy: Business strategy for extranets, intranets and the Internet.* MA: Butterworth-Heinemann.

Bock, G.E. & Marca, D.A. (1995). *Designing groupware: A guidebook for designers, implementors, and users* (p. 19). McGraw-Hill.

Chaturvedi, A. & Unhelkar, B. (2003). Composite business model in achieving enterprise application integration: A Web services perspective. *Proceedings of IBIM03 – International Business Information Management Conference*, Cairo, Egypt.

Coleman, D. (1995). Groupware technology and applications: An overview of groupware. In D. Coleman & R. Khanna (Eds.), *Groupware: technology and applications* (pp. 4-5). NJ: Prentice-Hall.

Day, J. D., & Zimmermann, H. (1983). The OSI reference model. *Proceedings of the IEEE, 71*, pp.1334-1340.

Gokhale, A., & Schmidt, D. (1998). Principles for optimizing CORBA Internet Inter-ORB protocol performance. *Hawaiian International Conference on System Sciences.*

Gromov, G. R. (1995). History of the Internet and WWW: Road 1 – USA to Europe, Retrieved from the World Wide Web at: *http://www.netvalley.com/netvalley/intval.html*

IBM WebSphere. (2002a). IBM. Retrieved March 22, 2002 from the World Wide Web at: *http://www-3.ibm.com/software/info1/websphere/platformoverview.jsp?S_TACT=102BBW01&S_CMP=campaign*

IBM Lotus Notes. (2002b). IBM. Retrieved April 9, 2002 from the World Wide Web at: *http://www.lotus.com/home.nsf/welcome/notes*

Kalakoa, R., & Whinston, A.B. (1997). *Frontiers of electronic commerce.* Addison-Wesley.

Laudon, K. C., & Laudon, J.P. (2002). *Management information systems: Managing the digital firm* (7th ed.). NJ: Prentice-Hall.

Laudon, K.C., and Laudon, J.P. (1993). *Business information systems: A problem-solving approach* (2nd ed., p. 5). FL: Dryden Press, Harcourt Brace.

Matsumura, M. (1997, November). Ultranet, the next network. *Java World.* Retrieved from the World Wide Web at: *http://www.javaworld.com/javaworld/jw-11-1997/jw-11-miko.html*

Microsoft. (2002a). C# introduction and overview. Microsoft Corporation. Retrieved March 26, 2002 from the World Wide Web at: *http://msdn.microsoft.com/vstudio/techinfo/articles/upgrade/Csharpintro.asp*

Microsoft. (2002b). Microsoft .NET: What is .NET? Retrieved March 26, 2002 from the World Wide Web at: *http://www.microsoft.com/net/defined/default.asp*

Microsoft. (2002c). Microsoft Exchange Server. Microsoft Corporation. Retrieved April 9, 2002 from the World Wide Web at: *http://www.microsoft.com/exchange/default.asp*

Microsoft TechNet. (1997). DCOM technical overview.

Monday, P.B. (2003). Web Services Architecture Patterns. Apress.

OMG. (2000a). Model driven architecture – Object management group white paper. Retrieved April 2, 2002 from the World Wide Web at: *ftp://ftp.omg.org/pub/docs/omg/00-11-05.pdf*

OMG. (2002b). Introduction to OMG specifications. Object Management Group Inc. Retrieved March 25, 2002 from the World Wide Web at: *http://www.omg.org/gettingstarted/specintro.htm#CORBA*

OMG. (2002c). Model driven architecture. Object Management Group Inc. Retrieved April 2, 2002 from the World Wide Web at: *http://www.omg.org/MDA*

OMG. (2002d). Model driven architecture. Retrieved April 2, 2002 from the World Wide Web at: *http://www.omg.org/mda/index.htm*

Palvia, S., Palvia, P. C., & Zigli, R. M. (1992). Global information technology environment: Key MIS issues in advanced and less-developed nations. In S. Palvia, P. Palvia, & R. Zigli (Eds.), *The global issues of information technology management.* Hershey, PA: Idea Group Publishing.

Perry, W. E., & Randall, R. W. (2002). *Surviving the challenges of software testing.* Dorset House.

Pfaffenberger, B. (1998). *Building a strategic extranet.* IDG books world-wide.

Sanjiv, K.R., Cantara, M., & Shetty, S. (2003). *Web services – Reality behind the Hype.* Web Services Webinar, Gartner Inc.

Shaw, M., & Garlan, D. (1996). *Software architecture: Perspective on an emerging discipline.* New York: Prentice Hall.

Shelly, G.B, Cashman, T. J., & Rosenblatt, H. J. (2001). *Systems analysis and design* (4th ed., Course Technology) (pp. 1.5-1.6). MA: Thomson Learning.

Sun. (2002a). Enterprise JavaBeans™ Technology. Sun Microsystems, Inc. Retrieved April 3, 2002 from the World Wide Web at: *http://java.sun.com/products/ejb/index.html*

Sun. (2002b). iPlanet – Home page. Sun Microsystems, Inc. Retrieved April 5, 2002 from the World Wide Web at: *http://iplanet.com*

Telstra. (2002a). Telstra BigPond broadband cable. Retrieved March 25, 2002 from the World Wide Web at: *http://www.bigpond.com/broadband/cable/products.asp*

Telstra. (2002b). Telstra high speed Internet and data service on ADSL. Retrieved March 26, 2002 from the World Wide Web at: *http://www.telstra.com.au/adsl/cbenef.htm*

Treese, G., Winfield, & Stewart L. C. (1998). *Designing systems for Internet commerce* (pp.83-85). MA: Addison Wesley Longman.

Unhelkar, B. (2003). Understanding collaborations and clusters in the e-business world. *We-B Conference,* Perth, Australia.

Wilson, M., Kannangara, K., Smith, G., Simmons, M., & Raguse, B. (2002). *Nanotechnology: Basic science and emerging technologies.* Australia: UNSW.

Endnotes

[1]   Coober Pedy – Opal Capital of the World. Retrieved from the World Wide Web at: http://www.cpcouncil.sa.gov.au/

[2]   Groupware is discussed in a later section in this chapter.

[3]   Data networks and open system communication, International Telecommunication Union.

[4]   S/MIME and OpenPGP, Internet mail consortium.

Chapter VI

Case Study in Globalization of Hospitals

In this chapter we discuss:

- The practical application of the entire GET process to a hospital
- How to transition this hypothetical hospital NSH to a Global Hospital
- A demonstration of how a consulting organization can handle the process of GET as it is applied to NSH, the hospital.

Importance of Tele-Health

This chapter demonstrates the application of the GET process in the area of Tele-health, to a hospital. The reason for selecting the domain of Tele-health for this exercise is significant. In the modern communication age, there are still many situations where people who are in pain and/or have an acute need for help have to travel hundreds of miles just to be close to a physician or a healthcare specialist. This scenario is exacerbated by overworked physicians and surgeons, and ever shrinking funds for health care from governments and other funding bodies. Thus the need for, and the value of, being able to provide medical facilities and support by utilizing technology is at its highest leading us to believe in the extreme importance of Tele-health in today's world. Tele-health is all about the use of technology to ease the ability to provide medical care beyond physical distances, especially in rural areas. Tele-health is also about alleviating the routine pressures on doctors beyond the needs of their own specialist or generalist skills. Tele-health goes further beyond patients and doctors, and also involves education, research and administration in the field of medicine. Given this tremendous importance of Tele-health, it is appropriate that the concepts of globalization discussed in this book, in all its previous chapters, are applied to a case study that deals with a hospital. In this chapter, we have appropriately considered the area of hospital management and patient access to care, in demonstrating the concepts of the GET process, as applied to a hospital. Needless to say, this remains a relatively small part of the overall effort required in globalizing a hospital. Nonetheless, we believe this is an excellent demonstration of most of the concepts discussed here. This chapter results from our attempts at verifying in practice the principles discussed in this book. Therefore, although the entire case study is hypothetical, it has its roots in a real life hospital, with real doctors, nurses, administrative staff, and of course, real patients. By considering the application of GET to Tele-health, we hope we will not only demonstrate the process to our readers, but also show how this process will come in handy in the health domain where globalization is going to become extremely important.

Case Study Statement

North-South Hospital (NSH) is a small hospital of about ten beds, with limited medical infrastructure, but extremely high niche expertise. It is located in one of the medium-sized cities in a developing nation, providing healthcare services. It is owned by a family (the husband being a renowned cardio-thoracic surgeon providing specialization in heart diseases and the wife, an internationally acclaimed neuro-physician, providing highly specialized treatment of neuro diseases). The hospital has no second-tier doctors and it operates on a skeleton staff of three to four nurses, a receptionist and an attendant who lives on the premises. The nurses operate on a roster basis, which means at any given time the hospital would have only two nurses available. Currently, NSH has a basic "informative" Web site that provides a brief profile of the hospital, its address, phone number and the contact details. The Web site does not have the ability to carry out any transactions at all, and does not have any links to other relevant sites. Thus, while the hospital has an electronic presence, it lives in isolation in a global sense.

The surgeon husband is in continuous demand all over the country. He travels by air and by road, to conduct diagnostics as well as curative surgeries, including open-heart operations, in some large cities where the necessary infrastructure for such complicated surgeries is available. The physician wife provides expertise in diagnosing and treating abnormalities in the brain, but for that she has to rely on the basic scanning equipment she has purchased for the hospital. Beyond that, she has to rely on infrastructure provided by bigger hospitals. However, because she is providing major consultations and, as a result, not traveling, she has to take greater responsibility for administration and management of the hospital. This becomes a challenge when she has to travel herself, presenting her own research and experience reports at national and international conferences. To add to their challenge, both doctors are gregarious in nature, with extremely active social lives through organizations such as the Rotary and a rich network of friends and family members spread out over the country and abroad who continuously seek their professional and personal assistance in medical matters.

Both owner doctors have realized the potential of the Internet in alleviating their situation. With the virtuous aim of not increasing their profits, but providing excellent service and freeing up time consumed by mundane tasks, they have decided to invest in the new technology. This, they hope, will not only alleviate their own stress in handling repeated and mundane tasks associated with medical and administrative procedures, but will also help them spread the wings of their expertise and go global.

Enactment of the GET process moves the organization from theory to practice, bringing into play the dynamics and the unknowns of globalization. This requires careful management of all practical aspects of the transition project including people, processes and technologies – the latter involving development and implementation of software systems. Thus, the skills and acumen of the people and teams in charge of these transitions become significant during this GET enactment. The earlier planning framework outlined in this book may be considered necessary for globalization, but it is certainly not sufficient. It is the ensuing enactment that makes the planning and documentation of the GET real. The enactment of the global transition is the execution of a sophisticated project that involves enormous skills and resources from all part of the organization. This requires each phase of the transition partitioned into small chunks of activities that can be easily managed, measured and assessed through the appropriate measurement protocols at predetermined checkpoints. The measurements will also provide information on the quality of the transition process as well as the success, or lack thereof, of the resultant global organization. The overall activities that form part of the enactment involve the following:

The very first practical aspect of enacting the globalization process is the launching of the process. This is the first "external" announcement by the organization that it is going global. The work done so far on the GET framework, in terms preparedness, planning and documentation is an invaluable starting point for enactment. During this early part of the enactment, the various socio-cultural-political aspects of globalization come into practice. This requires getting the external parties (including employees, customers and business partners) involved in the globalization process. Proper launch of the GET process will help in enticing this involvement from the external parties. And this involvement is important as, with GET enactment, the structure and behavior of the globalizing organization is bound to change – in turn affecting all internal and external parties that deal with the organization. And without their involvement and participation in the GET process during enactment, that enactment will not succeed. Due to the sheer importance of the launch, it is advisable to launch the transition through a steering committee, which is made up of various significant roles within the organization. While the exact composition of the committee can vary for different organizations, it is vital to include in the committee, customer representatives as well as representatives from business partners that will be affected by this transition. The timing of the launch of the global transition is also crucial and it depends upon the existing environmental situation including the current business, political and financial situation. In fact, during the launch, the organization moves into the mode of checking and re-checking the effect the transition is going to have on these partners as it moves forward with globalization. The launch, being the first step taken during enactment, plays an essential part in ensuring that the actual transition is as smooth as possible.

Methodscience Consulting

Enactment of Globalization, as discussed in Chapter IV, is the actual implementation of the *GET* process, for an organization. This enactment is akin to taking the actual "drive" in the *GET* process. When a real globalization process starts, it consumes time, money and resources. It is fraught with risks in all major areas of business such as finance, marketing and administration. More often than not, the small and medium enterprises, such as the NSH with specialist owner-doctors, do not have on-board skills to globalize themselves. Therefore, the owner-doctors (equivalent of a board in a medium to large business) have correctly taken the step of hiring a consulting company specializing in this area of work. We call this consulting company MethodScience Consulting (MS Consulting), with expertise in processes and process-architecture, including the GET process. This is the company meant to help NSH achieve the *Transition* of their *Enterprise.* MS Consulting is well versed in the *GET* process, and has expertise in implementing the process and helping globalize NSH hospital. Getting such external expertise is recommended in the very early phase of Enactment of the *GET* process. Following is a description of how the *GET* process is applied by MS Consulting to NSH hospital to achieve the aim of this small to medium enterprise to utilize the Internet and the technologies of globalization.

Goals and Vision of NSH

MS Consulting starts with two special workshop sessions with the owner-doctors, their own technology-savvy advisors, and an expert from the field of medical technology. This results in a better understanding of the current and future strategic vision for NSH, as well as the purpose of the project. This project goal is closely tied with the mission of NSH, which encompasses its direction, its core values, and its key offerings.

Mission

NSH hospital's mission is to provide globally accessible quality healthcare in the area of Cardio and Neuro diseases using state-of-the-art-technologies.

This mission statement requires the "buy-in" from all parties involved with the hospital. As NSH proceeds with GET, it will be necessary to refer to its mission and to those objectives that enable it to achieve its mission.

Objectives

Based on the aforementioned mission statement, and the desire of the owner-doctors to utilize the globalization technologies, the following were ascertained as the main objectives of the GET project, and the resultant system, for NSH:

- *To provide an easy to use and secure Web site for NSH hospital* – While NSH has a simple, informative Web site, it was ascertained that NSH should aim to provide excellent online healthcare services like booking, consultation, diagnosis, treatment, prescription and education anywhere at anytime through a specialized Web site. The Web site will be equipped with audio and video technology using high-speed connectivity resulting in spanning geographical distances.

- *To provide internal administration on the Web site* – Internal administration procedures and systems will have to be changed to Internet-based system to facilitate global management of the administration, rosters as well as most HR (Human Relations – People) functions.

- *To provide external alliances electronically* – NSH hospital's Web site should support supply chain with local as well as overseas pharmacies and drug suppliers. Interaction with government and other regulatory bodies should also be enabled electronically.

- *To provide a robust, reliable, flexible and secure IT infrastructure* – The Web site should be supported with encryption technology so that all users of the NSH Web site feel secure. Furthermore, all aspects of IT infrastructure need to be designed include network topology, database design, hardware and software components, security issues, and backup strategies. The design should also be flexible to allow easy update on the infrastructure.

Scope

MS Consulting outlined the scope of the globalization work to ensure that the aforementioned objectives are arrived at with efficiency and effectiveness. The focus of this project remains the development of a global-information-systems-based solution that will enable NSH to utilize the existing resources it has much better, and to enable it to compete globally. At the technical level, therefore, the solution covers re-engineering of business processes, conceptual design of an e-business system around a sophisticated Web presence, and hardware and software integration of the hospital's processes with the latest medical technologies in the fully secure environment. Furthermore, to prevent possible future damages, the scope of this work will also address the fallback procedures and backup strategies from both business and technology viewpoints. Finally, the scope of the GET transition will also encompass usability and training issues, which become particularly important when the users of the system are likely to be patients from all cross-sections of a developing country. Thus, in summary, following is a list encompassing the scope of the GET as applied to NSH:

- Focus on the mission and objectives of NSH from both current and future strategic viewpoint.

- Ensure NSH electronic capabilities to cater to medical services such as booking, consulting, diagnosis, treatment, prescription, education and administration.

- Approach the GET for NSH within an acceptable time frame for a small to medium enterprise.

- Ensure development of NSH relationships amongst its patients, nurses and suppliers both locally and globally.

- Develop an integrated supply chain system within NSH systems that will create and enhance organizations such as pharmacies and other hospitals to interact with NSH electronically.

- Develop NSH's growth and investment return strategy by outlining the financials of the project.

- Construct the human resources management systems to enrich the global employees' and global owner-doctors' capabilities.

- Create a market and territory for future products and services to be offered by this hospital.

- Incorporate the government regulations and required conditions into the business policies.

- Develop overall competitive advantage and its necessary capabilities for NSH.

Globalization of NSH – Practical Scenarios

We have discussed, in earlier chapters, the tremendous importance of communications in the modern world. According to a Gartner report quoted by Raskino (2001), by 2004, 60% of all business transactions are expected to be conducted on the Internet, and the Tele-health domain is no exception. Therefore, it is essential that NSH transitions into the electronic health domain as early as possible. With increasing impact of globalization, e-business is currently seen as the main drivers of change in the e-hospital marketplace. Strategically, therefore, the objective of NSH is no longer a question of whether or when to implement an e-business global strategy, but how and with whom. e-NSH is projected to enhance both NSH's internal and external activities.

Current SWOT

Here, we have a quick look at the SWOT of NSH, as it exists now.

Strengths:

- *Skills* – The owner-doctors are highly skilled at an international level, providing them with a unique and distinct advantage over other competitors.

- *Low Overheads* – Compared to other hospitals, NSH is a small hospital, with limited infrastructure. This is an advantage in terms of low overhead costs and, therefore, greater ease to change.

Weaknesses

- *Funds* – As with most small businesses, NSH has limited resources, requiring careful trade-offs between what to incorporate and what to leave off
- *Technical skills and infrastructure* – Both need to be developed for successful implementation of GET

Opportunites

Telemedicine – The telemedicine market is growing at a high rate, with developed nations having already implemented several projects and the technology becoming more and more economical by the day.

E-learning – This provides an opportunities for the owner-doctors to share their knowledge and expand their reach globally.

Threats

- *Infrastructure* – Due to the underdeveloped nature of the environment, it may be hard to implement some of the technological solutions in which reliability of the service is crucial.
- *Security issues* – There are several security issues which may hamper NSH from going global. Primary among these are privacy and confidentiality requirements of the patient's information.
- *Legal issues* – There may be several legal issues in different countries which will need to be taken into account before entering into global market.

SWOT after GET Process

The SWOT of e-NSH, after the application of GET process, will have the following highlights.

Strengths

- Improves customer relations
- Increases market share
- Provides better service quality
- Information availability
- Integrated collaboration within internal activities
- Integrated business processes, especially with external parties

Weaknesses

- Initial investment
- Technology inexperience

Opportunites

- Strategic alliances
- Research alliances
- Future growth in overseas markets
- Global reputation of NSH
- Cheaper medical facilities in developing nations

Threats

- Change management
- Larger hospital's implementations
- Socio-cultural issues

Changing Business Processes of e-NSH

Once the GET process is applied, and NSH transitions to e-NSH, there will be changes to the internal and external processes of the organization. This is reflected in the SWOT of the organization, as done above. We now summarize

Table 6.1. Enhancing NSH internal activities

Activities and Processes	NSH	Globalized e-NSH
Information analysis and availability	Information disseminate through different system, late evaluation of business performance	Faster information gathered and performance evaluation Deeper data classification
Introduction of standard procedures for shared operations within and among departments	In the paper based business environment, information sharing and collaboration among departments are not so effective	Enhance the use of shared information Effective collaboration among departments
Decision making process	Decision making is more centralized and the chance for employees to get involve in the decision making process is little	Enhanced because the system enables to concentrate the relevant information also in view of future project and budgeting

Table 6.2. Enhancing NSH external activities

Activities and Processes	NSH	Globalized e-NSH
B2B Operations	Not Available	SCM: pharmacy and medical equipment manufactures etc e-Procurement Video Conferencing Strategic alliances with Cardiac Centre Harapan Kita and Cipto Mangunkusumo Hospital
B2C Operations	Not Available	e-Prescription CRM e-Consulting
Information availability (for potential customers, clients, and business partners)	Poor and insufficient	Provides fast and complete information for customers through NSH informative web site, also e-consulting services. To communicate effectively with business partners and its alliances, NSH provides video conferencing functionalities.

the changes to the business processes of e-NSH. Table 6.1 compares internal processes of current NSH with those of e-NSH. Table 6.2 illustrates how e-NSH will improve NSH's external operations.

Requirements for Globalization

Once the mission and scope of globalization for NSH is understood, and once we have highlighted the major changes that will be undertaken when the internal and external business processes change, it is time to start documenting the requirements of the global entity, e-NSH, more precisely. This documentation requires conducting workshops and interviews – skills that are (and should be) readily available through MS consulting. The results of the workshops are recorded as follows:

1. Building a global e-hospital which uses state-of-the-art technology that enables the users to perform online healthcare services (e.g., e-booking, e-consultation, e-diagnosis, e-treatment and e-prescription) 24 hours a day, seven days a week, year round, and from anywhere in the world.

2. NSH will provide its patients as well as associated healthcare providers with convenient access to current and authoritative medical information on the Internet by providing easy, yet secured, access to information on consultation, diagnosis, treatment, prescription and education. By delivering medical information to the point-of-care, NSH will improve the quality of clinical outcomes.

3. Pre- and post-surgical activities that requires continuous support (especially for cardio-thoracic surgeries requiring long support after the operation) to be supported by special parts of the e-NSH Web sites.

4. Both physician and surgeon doctors will be made available for remote consulting through audio and video media using high-speed connectivity. This will enable them to easily expand their work outside of the country.

5. An IT project to create a substantial multi-media database complete with selected past consultations in audio and video forms will be made available to associated doctors, as well as select patients – particularly overseas patients who may have visited or been treated by the doctors.

6. Because of a wide age-group of potential users, all interfaces to the hospitals Internet-based systems will be designed keeping the usability concepts in mind.

7. A range of relative cross-functionalities (like sports information) will be included to attract non-patients to the site and keep them there, as well. This may help in keeping the community aware of the site.

8. Internal administrative systems (e.g., booking of consultation times, accounting of patients, or leave roster of nurses) will be moved to the Internet-based system to enable global (or off-site) management.

9. Potential links of the hospital's system to local and overseas drug suppliers to keep the inventories of medical supplies to the minimal within the hospital.

10. Software development and software maintenance be out-sourced based on a formal tendering process (which would include short and sharp promotion of the Request For Tender process within the country).

11. Consider the rapidly advancing new technologies (e.g., Mobile GRID technologies, Web services, etc.) to be incorporated in the technology strategies for e-hospital in the coming three to five years. This may require creative thinking on the part of MS consulting in suggesting how to use mobile technologies for NSH's external and internal processes. It is expected that incorporation of this technology will have positive repercussions for the "remote doctor" who may not be physically present or be available to cater to diagnostic-, treatment- and administration-related activities.

12. The supporting software system is expected to be available 24/7 to support NSH. In addition, a backup strategy should be well implemented, as it is important to provide a recovery plan in case of any breakdown.

13. The proposed solution will cover both business and information technology (IT) issues. Change management, Customer Relationship Management (CRM), marketing issues, and also security and legal Issues.

14. The system architecture will ensure robust network and data integration. The hardware and software components selected are the most reliable components among its range and also cost effective. Wherever feasible, wireless networks will be installed in order to reduce costs of physical infrastructure, as well as reduce disruption to existing operation of the hospital.

15. This proposal also recommends the structure of the e-NSH portal and the out-sourcing vendor who we believe is one of the best in the market. The global out-sourcing management methodology is also provided in the proposal.

16. This proposal will also ensure that it analyses and understands the global user, and provides strategies to attract patients and non-patient users to visit the e-NSH.

Having described the requirements resulting from workshops conducted by MS consulting, it should also be noted that in practical GET, these requirements will require formal documentation, perhaps using computer aided software engineering (CASE) tools. Many of these requirements will translate into critical requirements that need to be prioritized in consultation with the owner-doctors of the hospital. Here, we do not have the space to show in detail how these requirements can be documented within the software development methodological frameworks (These methodological aspects of software requirements and developments were mentioned towards the end of Chapter IV.). We do suggest that avid readers consult the software engineering books on this important aspect of global information systems (GIS).

NSH Core Business

NSH is specialized in cardiology and neurology. In order to compete competitively in the global market, NSH has to focus on its core business such as consultation, diagnosis, treatment, and education. In this stage, the technology development applied in the e-NSH is very important to enhance these core business sectors. Furthermore, NSH may use the Internet facilities to attract potential customers and generate the revenue in the core business sectors, as the Internet provides important information and convenience to all market segments.

Consultation

By going global towards e-business, NSH expands its consultation services into e-consultation. E-consultation is one of the core business to provide a "place" for patients to discuss medical issues with NSH experts, with the emphasis on the patients' convenience. Patients do not have to be present physically in the hospital. Instead, they can consult with NSH's doctors through both audio and video conferencing functionalities provided in NSH Web site.

Diagnosis

NSH is capable of providing a diagnosis from minor illnesses to major emergencies. Despite its expertise in cardiology and neurology, NSH is still able to provide services to patients with other diseases. This can be done by recommending the patients to partner doctors or hospitals. For some minor illnesses, NSH even can provide a diagnosis directly to the clients by conducting videoconferencing with partner medical experts asking for suggestions and opinions. In case of an emergency, NSH will transfer them to the appropriate medical facility.

Treatment

NSH specialized in both heart surgery and neurosurgery. Therefore, the treatment will focus more on heart and brain health services. Both heart and brain disease treatment will be crucial to the patients and the additional information is very useful to patients' health.

Diversified Business

NSH will enter the competitive market in the city and country where it exists. However, the global expansion toward the e-business is really important to increase the business efficiency. The diversification of e-NSH into various other avenues of service will be a part of the globalization process. This will easily result from creation of newer facilities as well as information libraries for medical students on the e-NSH Web sites.

Health Services

The main objective of NSH in the community is to provide health services in the region where it exists. While the NSH specialized services are heart and brain surgery, the hospital will strive to provide excellence in these services comparable with the larger hospitals, and in some cases even better – due to the personalized nature of the services.

Prescription

While prescribing medicines is an integral part of NSH business, application of GET will provide a more convent way for patients to get drugs from leading pharmacies. Doctors in NSH will create an e-prescription file for particular patient and record it into the database for future reference. Patients may use the e-prescription to purchase medicine from NSH's alliance pharmacies. This service can be made available through the e-NSH portal.

Education

Online library access will become an adequate resource for anyone. The main purpose is to provide a way to access useful health information on the Web. Users are expected to get a wide range of information and research on health care, such as the diseases, drug guide, and medical test or even search for any information on medicine's topics from journals and articles. NSH health sciences library is designed to deliver expert medical information to providers and patients at the point-of-care in order to help providers take better care of their patients and help patients live a healthier life.

Global NSH User Classifications

One of the most important aspects of GET is understanding and analyzing the user groups. Since these user groups of a GIS are likely to be spread across physical, time and cultural distances, it is important to consider them right at the outset of the GET process. In case of NSH, the following are groups of potential users identified to be the main users of the proposed system.

The Patient

The patient, and the potential patient, is at the heart of e-NSH's user groups. This is because it is the patient that is meant to be served by the hospital and, therefore, the patient should be provided with the utmost facilities when it comes to globalization. We may analyze the patient-user in terms of their needs, in terms of the gravity of their situation, pre- or post-operative care, and type of support required, to name but a few. For example, a patient requiring general information on how to keep up with breathing exercises after a heart-lung operation is less urgent than a patient who is being transported to the hospital via an ambulance.

Some of the advantages patient-users will realize by accessing e-NSH through its GIS include:

- Awareness of the name of the doctor and his/her skills and profile
- As far as possible, a detailed description of the standard structure of the fees likely to be charged
- Availability of the doctor in terms of days and timings, also resulting in time saving in terms of appointments, cancellations and re-schedulings
- Avoiding of overcrowding in day-time consultations
- Instructions to be followed before testing or consulting
- Have a chance to discuss some part of the problem before the appointment with a junior/support doctor, possibly via e-mail

The Owner-Doctors Specialists

The proposed system will change the way both physicians and specialists conduct health care services:

- Accessible anytime from anywhere through the NSH Web site in order to eliminate geographical distances
- The Web site could help physicians and specialists in providing medical diagnosis, treatment, prescription and education
- Provide remote consulting via audio and video media in high-speed connectivity
- Ease of use and only requiring minimal computer skill or training
- Real-time information update
- Knowledge of their schedules from anywhere in the country or even the world
- Knowledge about the history of the patient or his problem and documentation of all necessary information
- Secured access

- Can spend more time using their medical skills rather than administrative skills

Nurses

- Ease of use in supporting nurses' works with self-explanatory interface
- Integration between medical devices to provide better and faster medical services
- Allow information access such as patient records and roster schedule
- Ease of rostering

Administration Staff

- All NSH staffs, including receptionist, attendant and technical staff
- For receptionist, the proposed system should create simple Web-based administrative management featuring online booking of consultation times, billing statement and nurses working and on leave
- For attendant, the proposed system should support and allow easy access to any non-medical related activities
- For technical staff, the proposed system is required to be reliable, flexible and secure. In addition, the proposed system should be easy to maintain, providing minimal technical problems and making it possible for immediate recovery

Suppliers (e.g., Pharmacies)

The proposed system could improve the inventories of medical supplies within the management of the hospital as it will deal electronically with "business partners" of e-NSH. Since NSH deals with many companies in the delivery of hospital-related materials, goods, or services, if these functions can be transferred to the global information systems supporting e-NSH, the administrative pressure on the hospital will be drastically reduced.

Government Agencies

Electronic governance is a crucial and integral part of the globalization process of any organization. Therefore, it is essential that e-NSH systems are linked electronically to government bodies, whenever convenient. E-NSH will therefore interact with the local and state government bodies dealing with Telehealth, in complying with health, security and welfare issues. E-governance will also help e-NSH deal with the statutory legal requirements in terms of notification of diseases, deaths in hospitals, and coroner's inquiries, if required. Finally, the accounting and taxation issues dealing with administration of the hospital can also be handled by GIS.

NSH Change Management

As soon as the requirements for the e-NSH start being implemented, the MS consulting firm managing this GET process will have to start handling change. Although the planned GET implementation will span a period ranging from six months to a year, it is essential that the change is planned and managed from the beginning right through to the end of the transition. Some of the key techniques that will be used in managing the change will include:

- Training – for the doctors, nurses, staff members and most importantly the patients.

- Communication – The communication used previously would need to be adapted to the changing situation and the parties involved.

- Recognition and Reward – Patients could receive some incentive, besides the obvious, for adopting the new methods. Staff should also be rewarded or held responsible for their actions.

- Right structure – The correct structure would need to be implemented to enforce the new system. This would include assigning the correct authority with the correct responsibilities.

- Phasing – The change would need to be adopted in phases so that the stakeholders involved may gradually familiarize themselves.

Figure 6.1. NSH change management structure

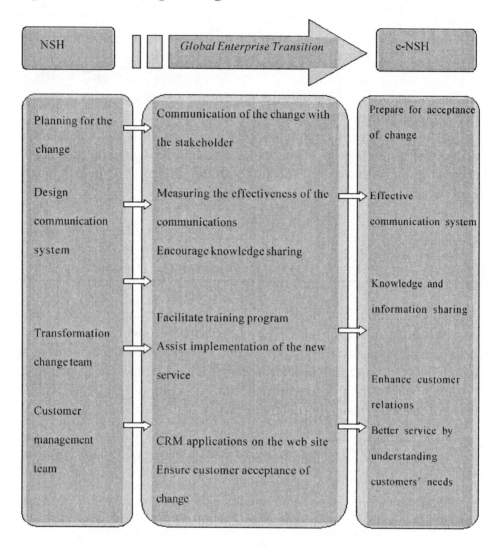

It is recommended that NSH conduct and develop five steps of change management to make sure the transition from NSH to e-NSH goes smoothly. These include planning for the change, designing the new communication system, and developing the transformation change team, customer management team, and integration team as shown in Figure 6.1.

Step 1. Planning for the Change

Good planning is undoubtedly very important to the success of the transformation process. Therefore, NSH management has to carefully plan the change within the transformation process. To achieve that, NSH will have to undertake a capability evaluation, which includes financial capability to go global and also the capability of NSH to survive in the face of current e-hospital market competition. Furthermore, it is extremely important that the planned changes are communicated to all stakeholders, which includes doctors, nurses, administration staff and patients.

Step 2. Communication

What must be considered in this step is measuring the effectiveness of the communications and also encouraging the knowledge sharing culture within NSH. One of the strengths of e-NSH is to provide an effective communication system. By providing a "place" for employees to share information and knowledge, more efficient and effective collaboration among departments can be achieved.

Step 3. Change Management Team

A sub-team dealing with crucial change management aspects like training in changing business processes will be invaluable in managing this change. This team may also provide technical support such as how to use the software, how to share the information and knowledge, communicate effectively through the system, and so on and so forth. Furthermore, the team will assist employees in implementing the new service to NSH's customers such as e-prescription, e-registration, etc. Without the formation of a change management team responsible for smoothing out the change process, it is likely that the costs of integration and training may increase.

Step 4. Customer Management Team

Formation of this team is helpful when it comes to implementation of e-CRM applications on the Web site, ensure customer acceptance of the change and also to educate the customer how to use and collaborate with the new system. The team aims for enhancing the relationships with customers as well as providing better service quality by more understanding of customers' needs.

Step 5. Integration Team

The Integration Team is responsible for forming alliances with pharmacy, medical experts, and other hospitals in the region. The Integration Team aims to successfully manage the supply change management to achieve an effective integration with NSH's suppliers. The ability to integrate systems including both internal and external processes will prove pivotal, as each layer of the organization will need to be morphed into a complete e-business model.

The team will also responsible in project outsourcing management by conducting appropriate reviews and inspection on project development and make sure the project is going well, on time, and matches every single requirement in the project plan. Furthermore, the team assists the global outsourcing teams to create a global sharing library, and some standards including modeling, process, database, language, and quality standards to be used by the global outsourcing contractors around the world.

Major NSH Change Considerations

In addition to the five steps mentioned earlier, it is worth mentioning the practical issues in dealing with the change that will affect NSH.

Keeping NSH Owner-Doctors Consensus

Change management, within the NSH context, requires maintenance of complete executive consensus during enactment. This is vital to enactment as, without consensus and support from the owner-doctors, the GET process may not succeed. It is vital that the doctors have a clear understanding of the globalization strategy and have recognized the implications of enacting the global transition process. Lack of this understanding and the resultant discord is one of the highest risks to the globalizing organization. Practical suggestions in the context of NSH include:

- Communication amongst the doctors in terms of e-NSH progress.
- Communicating the changes with the internal employees and external business partners.
- Electronic and physical means of communication should be utilized.
- Regular committee meetings between the owners and MS consulting should be organized to ensure tracking of progress.

Managing Resources

There is a need to manage the people, information and infrastructure resources during application of GET to NSH. Managing these three categories of resources are the essential and critical components in the company's global transition project and they are further expanded below:

- *People* – the MS consulting staff, as well as the doctors, nurses and administration staff involved in the transition need to be managed properly. It is imperative during the enactment of GET that there are sufficient personnel available to initiate and manage the transition. Their timely availability and commitment will be vital to achieve e-NSH. The identification and management of development teams for the software applications to be used by e-NSH is also an important part of managing this resource.

- *Information* – related to NSH, as well as information needed by the transitioning personnel comes under this heading. Details related to the usage of the GIS by users, especially overseas users, is a crucial part of this information gathering and dissemination.

- *Infrastructure* – this resource includes the hardware as well as the available development environment for e-NSH. Furthermore, changes to even the basic infrastructures, such as phones and faxes, computer servers and workstations, computer peripherals (printers, scanners), network components (hubs, routers and cables), and backup equipment would form part of this resource.

Managing Time and Budgets

Management of crucial (and limited) time and budgets is important for the success of e-NSH. This will require the detailed plan, as described earlier, and management of budgets. An example budgetary plan is provided later in this chapter, as a benchmark for GET at this level of business. Also, in practice, it is essential to ensure that the timing and budgets are continuously revised based on the time and money spent "thus far." Finally, due to the involvement of numerous external parties and possible alliances during GET, it is essential to update all these parties in terms of the time and budgets relevant to them.

The New Global NSH E-Business

The market of NSH business is competitive and the business orientation is focused on the e-hospital health services. The large increase in Internet users will lead to an attractive market in which to compete. Globalization becomes very important to increase business effectiveness. Technology development is very crucial in providing opportunities to the organization.

The potential emerging businesses for NSH in the near future include logistic services for e-business and e-commerce, and integrated business logistics providing end-to-end services, including warehousing and inventory management.

E-Consultations

Consulting is one of the most fundamental processes undertaken by NSH, especially by the physician or doctor who has to examine and diagnose patients in order to provide treatment. In cases where the patients are unable to physically come to see the doctor, or in an extended family-and-friend scenario, where the owner-doctors are obliged to see to patient outside the hospital, considerable time is spend in travel. With GET, the global NSH will have processes for consultation that use a combination of physical meeting as well as electronic consultation. It is proposed that the doctors should be able to make use of video-conferencing and related technologies in order to view the diagnostic features and tests of the patient, and be able to ascertain the state of the patient before insisting on either party undertaking the travel to be in physical presence. The doctors can see the reports of the patients such as the ultrasound report, etc., through the high speed connectivity arrangement. After looking at the reports he can advise on the patient's situation and the kind of treatment required. The patients can seek the doctor's advice through the e-hospital's Internet services. This can be done thought the intensive use of the hospital Web site and the mail services offered by the site. The patients can contact the doctor anytime and the doctors can respond to their queries from any part of the world. Finally, as the sophistication of the NSH global site increases, it is envisioned that the surgeon will be able to view as well as project operations happening remotely.

The advantage of this e-consulting process will invariably free up time for the doctors, saving on otherwise wasted traveling time and fatigue in reaching patients in the remote regions. Furthermore, this process will make the expertise of these renowned doctors available to patients overseas, anywhere and at anytime. However, high speed connectivity and large bandwidth required for transmission of the kind of video and audio data on the Internet remains a major challenge to this process.

E-Appointments and Scheduling

Current Set-Up

* The present way is not much advanced and basically depends on personal visiting or calling on the phone. When a patient visits he gets a serial number, where he is placed in the line going for a check up when his number comes. On busy days this creates a lot of overcrowding, as patients don't know how much time they need to wait. Appointments made over the phone almost reflect the same, but the patients know where they are and at what time they have their appointment. Based on that they come to the clinic for their scheduled check up. The only advantage with this is it avoids overcrowding.

Limitations

- Takes up a lot of time spent waiting. No fixed consultation time is given.
- Patients get irritated and feel inconvenienced, as they don't know or are not given any instructions about the things they must do before check up.
- Completely illiterate about doctor skills.
- Tied to do things, as they don't have lot of options.

Proposed Solution

The only way to avoid all the above complications is by automation of the process. An automated process allows the patient to access the Web site, login, enter his user name and password, browse the appointment schedule, match it to his availability, send a request, get confirmation, enter all the details, include personal doubts (if any), pay, get the address, and receive the instructions to be followed prior to his appointment.

The system going to be implemented is based on the above structure and creates a highly secured environment. A patient visits the Web site and if he is an existing member, he logs in with his user ID and password. If he is not a member, he registers himself and gets confirmation. Once he is logged in, he can browse through a lot of options. A patient selects timing convenient to him and confirms it by paying the consultation fee. Unless and until the minimum fee is paid, the appointment is not confirmed.

Prescription Management

Current Set-Up

- When diagnosing a patient, the doctor writes down his medicine doses on a pad nearby and then the nurse checks on it and gives the required dosage to the patient.
- The patient has to seek out the doctor time and again to check on his prescription after he has left the hospital.

Limitations

- The nurse has to be at continuous vigilance to keep track of the patients.
- The doctor does not have much time to be available to all patients for their prescription advice.

Proposed Solution

There will be a "prescription portal" set up near the bed of the patients that will allow the doctor to enter the updates of each patient and his daily medicinal doses. When the doctor has finished entering the information, the central system will be updated along with the database. The nurses will be given a handheld device. The system will have a record of the nurses on duty and then send a message to the handheld device of the corresponding nurse and inform about the patient's name and his dosage for the day.

The patients will be given a unique log in on the hospital Web site. When the patient wants to contact the doctor about his prescription, he can contact the doctor through Internet services. When the doctor will respond to this query, the prescription along with the new medical advice will give the patient the location of the pharmacy nearby so that the patient does not have to search for the pharmacy. This will be done with the help of the details that are stored on the system. When the doctor is sending a prescription, he will click on some button that will activate the search. With the database records of the patient and the stored records of the pharmacies, the prescription will include the location of the pharmacy as well. When the patient accepts the prescription he will get an option for accepting the invoice from the corresponding pharmacy. If he accepts the service of that pharmacy, the invoice of the prescription will be given to the patient so that he may know exactly how much he has to pay. And in the end the patient can go and fetch his medicines from that store.

Advantages/Benefits

- Saves times and makes the hospital operating system more organized.
- Give patients the convenience to refer to their doctor at any time.
- Informs the patient about the nearest store and relieves him of finding the store for himself.

- Automatic updating of the prescription records of the patient. There is no need for the operator to enter the details of the prescription.

Issues

- A large set-up of the pharmacy and hospital links have to be put together.
- The nurses and the staff have to be provided with separate handheld devices.
- The patients have to be informed about the above proposed facility.

Electronic Patient Records

Current Set-Up

- The medical history and the records of patients are maintained manually on files.
- One of the staff members has to update the records of the patients whenever a new statement occurs.

Limitations

- The records which are stored in files are difficult to access.
- Attention has to be paid for preserving the records and the paperwork for sometime.
- The patient does not have an exclusive access to his own medical proceedings.
- It is not easy for the doctor to retrieve any of the medical proceedings any time for further consultation.

Proposed Solution

When a patient enters the hospital, all his details will be entered in the central computer system. This will then be further updated as and when required by the authorized person and will automatically update the corresponding information in the database.

The records will be accessible anytime from anywhere. Once the person logs onto the hospital Web site, he will be able to see any information about anyone if he/she has the authority to do so. The patient will have exclusive right to view his own history.

For educational and further reference purposes, the operations and the consultations will be audio- and video-recorded. This recording will also be stored electronically. So when desired by the doctor he can refer to his previous activities. For education purposes (See section Education), the records will be retrieved and then shown to students.

Advantages/Benefits

- Easy access to records and operation proceedings for further reference.
- Maintenance of electronic records is much easier than handling manual ways of storage.

Issues

- Patient's consent required before their video-recorded activities are shown to students and for other educational purposes.
- An additional staff member required to enter and update the records.
- Large hardware storage device required to hold such enormous data chunks.

Billing and Payments

Current Set-Up

- The present process is completely running manually on paperwork, which consists of maintaining all the details of the services provided such as consultation fees, medicines issued, lab tests conducted, bed charges/accommodation charges, food and beverages charges, etc., handled by a receptionist. Payment procedure is followed in the following way where the receptionist gives the bill to the client which is paid in the form of cash or cheque.

Proposed Solution

All the above process will be automated where the manual approach for billing and payments will be automated to e-billing and e-payments. For every patient, an ID will be created and which has access to all of his account details. Once logged into this account, it can have access to:

- Charges involved in diagnosis.
- Billing and payment history online.
- Informing an authorized person to pay his bill.
- Viewing and paying his bills online.
- A detailed description of the services offered.

Consumer Benefits/Overall Advantages

- Convenient and easy.
- Optimizing inventory management.
- Saves a lot of time, so the patient or the receptionist does not need to wait for the bill or to update the bill, or need to stand in the line to pay the bill or transfer the cheque in the bank.
- Maintains privacy and is completely secured for both client and the hospital management.
- Online history of e-bills and e-payments can be maintained.
- Available around the clock for 24 hours a day, seven days a week, and can be accessed from any part of the world via the Web services.
- No accounting hassles as this runs electronically.

Issues

When running manually (the present situation):

- Keeping patient records updated manually with the current bills for in-the-door patients.
- Time factor.
- Costs involved in mailing the bill to the patient.
- Account hassles/mistakes in calculations.
- Inconvenience to the patient if he doesn't have enough money to pay his bill.
- Posting it to the wrong address.

With an automated process:

- Customers may or may not be able to afford the technical devices used for the service provided.
- It takes a lot of time for training and getting used to the new system and devices.
- Security issues.

Payroll

Current Set-Up

- As already mentioned the entire process running is working manually. Daily the staff that works signs in the staff ledger as soon as they come into work and signs out when they finish their work at the end of the day. At the end of the week the ledger is checked and working hours of the staff is calculated and pay is calculated according to their hourly pay. This is forwarded to the management who prepares the cheques for them and cheques are issued on the next working day.

Proposed Solution

The complete system is automated. Every staff member is given a hand held devices with a unique code which is linked with the sensor and then to the database. As the nurse enters the hospital for work the sensor detects the device which has a unique code. The sign-in time is automatically recorded in the database. In the same way, it detects the code when the staff is signing out after finishing the work. With the information in the database the worked hours are calculated by the system itself. Based upon the hourly rate of the individual, their wages are calculated. This is finalized and forwarded to the doctor who approves it. And the wages are deposited into their respective accounts through online banking from the hospital's operating budget.

Advantages/Overall Benefits

- A lot of time is saved and staff can work on different areas in that time.
- Avoids unnecessary problems like calculation mistakes in counting hours and wages.
- Employee satisfaction is highly achieved. Wages can be paid on time.
- Can be accessed globally and managed.

Inventory Management

Current Set-Up

- The entire inventory is managed manually where a stock taker keeps checking the record of the availability of drugs and figures it every day.
- Based on that record, all the orderings are made. The supplier gets the order through phone and arranges for delivery. The bills are given when the order is dispatched and delivered. Payments are processed later when time permits.

Limitations

- Errors in calculations.
- Fixed and limited sources of suppliers. If the stock is available with the supplier the hospital gets it or else this creates a lot of tension finding its availability elsewhere.
- Do not have a clear knowledge of the expired drugs in the store as it is not possible to check each and every drug.
- Mistakes in ordering.
- Time consuming.
- Paper-based work in billing and payment.

Proposed Solution

All the systems are interrelated to each other. We have a bar code for each and every drug which is recorded in the database. As the drug is taken out from the stock room or the pharmacy, it is scanned by a barcode scanner. This updates the records in the database.

This keeps track of stock balance, items below safety stock, items with due expiry dates, excess stock of items, etc. At the end of every day a request is sent to the manufacturer or the dealer. The dealers send the quotation of the drugs and are delivered as soon as all the formalities are satisfied.

Advantages/Benefits

- Accurate and secure product identification, meaning zero errors in identifying the right product.
- Completely secure.
- Improves the contacts and quotations from different manufacturers.
- Reduction in administrative work where they can spend more time for patients.
- Quicker reaction leading to more satisfied customers whether these are external or internal.
- Fewer mistakes meaning lower costs of operations.

- Improved stock management where space is reduced for storing and increase in operating capital availability.
- Work can be properly organized and unnecessary tensions can be avoided.
- More efficient operations through optimized flow of products, information and improved utilization of assets.

Emergency Case Handling

Current Set-Up

- The hospital depends on bigger hospitals for major operations.
- There are no second-tier doctors in the hospital.
- There are only ten beds in the hospital.
- The staff is not big.
- The doctors are sometimes away from the hospital on other operations in some other cities.
- The problem statement does not say anything about the hospital ambulance. (We assume that the hospital does not have this facility.)

Limitations

- The hospital in unable to attend to emergency cases.
- Small staff will not be able to attend to a large number of patients in case of an emergency.
- The patients coming in under an emergency cannot be given attention from the doctors.
- The hospital cannot react to a major calamity due to its small staff and unavailability of doctors.
- The patients cannot be transferred immediately to bigger hospitals.

- If the hospital gets a call for ambulance, they cannot respond, as they do not have their own ambulance.

Proposed Solution

The hospital system will have a database of all the doctors who can visit the hospital in case of emergency. In case of an emergency case, the staff will retrieve the database and contact the doctor. In return, the doctor will respond whether the doctor can come there immediately. If not then the next available doctor will be contacted.

The hospital staff will have access to bigger hospitals' ambulance services. If the patient is under the need of immediate attention or require an immediate operation and can't wait for the doctor's arrival then the staff will be authorized to make a direct call to the ambulance of the bigger hospital. This will be accomplished with the system alerts that will be directly linked to the bigger hospital. The alert message will have the number of patients that are to be transferred. As soon as the bigger hospital receives this emergency alert call, they will send their ambulance with a doctor to fetch the patient. A doctor will also accompany the ambulance. In this way, the patient could get immediate medical treatment if required.

If the ambulance of that hospital is busy or the number of patients is more than the ambulance can carry, then the hospital will contact the other hospital allies for the emergency ambulance service. In this way the chain will continue until the conditions are met.

In the meantime, the doctors in the bigger hospitals can guide the staff to take the necessary steps. This can be done with the help of high speed connectivity video-conferencing. The doctors at the other end will be able to see and hear the patient's condition and tell the staff about the precautionary steps.

Any call coming in for an ambulance will be attended and the same course of action will be taken. The staff will take down the details of the location and via the same alert messaging, the location will be specified to the bigger hospital. The ambulance will then directly go to that location and fetch the patient. Depending on the condition of the patient, the doctor who accompanies the ambulance will decide where the patient should be taken.

Advantages/Benefits

- The hospital overcomes its drawback of reacting to emergency case handling.
- The doctors can get an immediate message in case of an emergency.
- The patient can be transferred to the bigger hospital if it is required without much delay.
- The chance of unavailability of an ambulance and the doctor get ruled out. Because if one is not available, then the other is contacted through the reaction chain.
- The patient is assured of an immediate treatment. (By the video-conferencing method and ambulance-doctor service.)
- Even if the hospital is running at its full capacity, the patient will not be turned down due to unavailability of beds. He will be transferred to the bigger hospital.

Issues

- To accomplish the critical chain of hospital emergency service, a lot of effort has to be put in. Forming alliances with the bigger hospital and the bigger hospital with the other hospitals will require a lot of time and counseling.
- For the video-conferencing and alert messages high speed connectivity will be required.
- To implement the above idea, Web services would be required and there are certain issues regarding the implementation of Web service which are still not clear. For example, the owner of the Web service, the designing issues, etc., still need to be considered.

Education

Current Scenario

- The problem statement does not state anything about the educational programs carried about by the hospital or the doctors.
- However, the doctors are consulted by their network of friends and relatives for medical advice.

Limitations

- The doctors are limited to the network of peer and senior doctors.
- The doctors are deprived of having knowledge about new talents and emerging skills in the field.
- They are unable to pass on their knowledge and practical experience to the junior doctors.
- Since both the doctors are renowned, the new doctors would like to learn from their highly acclaimed experience. This is not feasible due to the tight schedule of the doctor in the present scenario.

Proposed Solution

The doctors do not have enough time to attend student seminars and give lectures to them. The junior doctors can gain from the experience of the doctors with the help of the multimedia database that will be maintained by the hospital. All the operations that are done by the doctors will be recorded. After the operation, the doctor concerned will give a short lecture in his free time that will be recorded along with the operation proceeding in the same computer file. So when the tape plays, the voice of the doctor will also be played.

When a student group comes in for a lecture, the tape will play and the student can understand what exactly is happening in the operation.

Apart from this, there will be distance education programs. In this manner, the doctor will be connected through high speed connectivity technology and he can deliver lectures to the student in some other city or place. To show examples of his operation he can retrieve the operation recording from his database and display it online. It will be a video-conferencing where both the parties can interact simultaneously.

Some of the authorized doctors from other hospitals and countries will also be able to view the works of the doctors for consultation purpose.

Advantages/Benefits

The doctor's skill does not remain confined to him only.

Issues

- For video-conferencing high speed connectivity has to be maintained.
- For storing the recording of an entire operation a large space will be required. The operations recorded will have certain date limit. After that date the recordings will be deleted due to storage issues.
- For security and privacy issues the records will have only authorized admittance.

Pre-Operation Briefing

Current Scenario

- When a patient is admitted he has to be monitored for his body behaviors like blood pressure and temperature. The patient details are kept on traditional papers pads.
- The doctor has to go through the details of the patient before any operation. For this, the doctor utilizes the paper records of the patient.

Limitations

- The staffs have to maintain the paperwork of the patient.
- It is difficult to keep track of all the patients via paperwork.
- The doctor has to spend some more time in reading about the patient's history and details.

Proposed Solution

When the patients get admitted to the hospital, his details will be entered in his record in the computer. Details about previous operations, results of various medical tests, etc., will be stored in the computer. From that day forward, until the date of operation, his daily medical details like the blood pressure, temperature, etc., will also be entered in the computer system. These details will be provided to the doctor directly on his system or any hand held device he would carry.

When the doctor is about to go for the operation he will connect to his system. There would be special headphone kind of device that will be connected to the system wirelessly. When the doctor clicks on the patient's name the system, with the help of voice recognition software, will read the patient's details to the doctor. While the recital is going on the doctor can relax and listen to the patient's medical details.

Otherwise, the doctor will also be able to get the details on his handheld device. Through mobile connections, all the details will come to the handheld when the doctor is on the way to the operation. In the meantime the doctor can read out the records and get familiar with the patient.

Advantages/Benefits

- The headache of maintaining cumbersome paperwork gets waived off.
- The doctor can actually relax before going for the operation.
- It saves the time of the doctor if he has to travel some distance.
- The time that would be otherwise be wasted will be utilized.

Issues

- This type of arrangement assumes the extremely busy schedule of the doctor.
- Mobile technologies play a major rule in the implementation of such a pact.

Staff Management

Current Scenario

- The hospital is short-staffed.
- It has three to four nurses who work on a shift basis.
- No second-tier doctors.
- The hospital has a receptionist and an attendant.
- The shift-based nurses use a paper-based technique to keep track of their shifts and hours worked.

Limitations

- Keeping track of the shifts involves signing in daily and having to manually record the hours worked.
- Similarly, the receptionist would have no time due to additional tasks like maintaining inventory, handling patient calls, coordinating the doctor's appointments, maintaining records and so on.
- The attendant would do miscellaneous jobs like physically receiving and stocking the medicine. He/she also helps in other ad-hoc tasks that may turn up from time to time.

Proposed Solution

- Automate and re-engineer the entire process of maintaining staff records. Integrate this with the payroll and all other systems so that hours are calculated and payments are made automatically. This would be done using mobile devices.

- Each nurse will be given a PDA equipped with a sensor and a unique code which is connected to the central system. The sensor will detect when the nurse arrives and leaves the hospital. This way the nurses' working hours can be automatically recorded.

- They are given a detailed description of their work for that day into their PDA every morning such as their place of working, patients they are dealing with, necessary items they should take for every case, instructions to be given to the patient, exact timings of the operations, and if the physician needs their assistance. This helps to plan themselves and avoids unnecessary tensions.

- Every nurse can update the patient medical record in the central system after they visit each ward such as the patient's blood pressure, heart rate and all the needed tests before the physician come to visit the patient.

- Similarly this PDA will also have calendar features, so that when outside the hospital, they can connect to the Internet and update their roster. In case a nurse wants to apply for a leave she can send a request for the leave from their PDA and receive the approval or rejection on their device. In a serious condition if a staff member is suffering from sudden illness, he can inform his colleagues via SMS to replace him.

- The sensor is already attached to the central system and their unique codes allow tracing their locations. This in case of emergency work can be sent onto their PDAs to notify whoever the one is nearest to the location.

Advantages/Benefits

- The employees have time for other important jobs. They don't have to keep monitoring their shifts and duties.

- Create a systemic lifestyle.

- Improves efficiency and accuracy of work performed.

- Global access on the information and works allocated for the staff and the doctors to know who is working and on what. If necessary guide them and attach some more work needed in their flow.

- This will also enable them to respond to emergency calls.

- Avoids unnecessary confusion.
- Updating the record in the central system allows doctors also to monitor peculiar cases continuously in their schedule.
- Improve better communication, which will be done very easily in passing information and getting help.

Issues

- To utilize the benefits from the new structure, the staff is required to undergo a thorough training.
- Extensive use of expensive gadgets will lead to high implementation costs.
- High speed connectivity would be required.

Patient Monitoring

Current Scenario

- The hospitals currently monitor patients' vital signs using an ECG, which prints results on a light-sensitive paper.
- This information is not stored electronically. This poses a major limitation to the doctors.

Limitations

- Because of the current monitoring methodology, the staff can only monitor the patient when at the hospital.
- Since this is a small hospital, the doctors frequently have to travel to meet their not-so-critical patients. While away a nurse monitors for any discrepancy and then pages the doctor.

Proposed Solution

The new system would record vital sign indicators on a computer, meaning a patient's records could be easily accessed at any time and from anywhere via the Internet. There is already a similar system in place which was developed by researchers from Griffith University's School of Microelectronic Engineering and School of Applied Psychology, in conjunction with students taking part in the University's Industrial Affiliates Program which connects industry with Griffith students.

The system could have an SMS alert sent automatically to their mobile phone when a patient's readings were out of the ordinary, potentially cutting down the time it would take to respond to a medical emergency.

In addition, electrodes connected to the body feed information into a small device which could be carried around by a patient. The readings monitored by this device could then be transmitted via a mobile phone or a secure Internet link directly to the doctor or hospital.

There are already several systems available in the market which enable remote monitoring of the patient from the comfort of their homes. (See http://www.longtermcarelink.net/frames/fm_find_remote.html.)

Advantages/Benefits

Benefits to Doctor

- This will provide more mobility for medical practitioners.
- The doctors can move around with a free mind as they know they will can get immediate results.
- Analysis of the patient's vital signs' history can be done quickly.

Benefits to Patient

- The patient will have confidence in being monitored while away from the hospital.

- Reduces unnecessary visits to doctor's offices.
- Provides education to the patient in early symptom management.
- Quicker discharge from the hospital after surgery.

Issues

- The cost of developing such a network will be very high.
- This aspect requires training, not only for the employees, but also for patients.
- The Infrastructure has to be built accordingly.
- Security/privacy issues.

(See: http://www.electroline.com.au/elc/feature_article/item_112002b.asp.)

Audio-video-based remote-patient monitoring via the Internet raises privacy issues that only clearly defined confidentiality and authentication requirements for secure Internet communication can address. MPEG compression technologies can transmit high-quality audio-video via the Internet so that a family member can use an office PC or wireless mobile terminal to monitor a bedridden patient's image and vital signs while a caregiver runs errands. However, such systems raise privacy concerns. Transmitting unprotected audio-visual signals, compressed in a standard format, over the Internet carries the risk that someone can monitor these transmissions, accidentally or intentionally. For medical and health care applications, security issues in the Internet's transport and network layers cause the most concern. Although encryption can protect data, using such technology for remote-patient monitoring should not compromise Internet accessibility and performance. Patient-monitoring applications require excellent performance and quality of service to provide accurate live information to the monitoring side. Thus, the performance of the end-to-end Internet infrastructure itself must be the subject of future study. (See: http://www.computer.org/computer/co2001/r5024abs.htm.)

Technological Aspects of Remote Monitoring

- See: http://www.imtc.gatech.edu/projects/biotech/ehc_patent5.html; http://www.nasiff.com/vitals.htm; http://www.nasiff.com/main.htm; http://www.cybernetmedical.com/files/applicationsofmedstar.pdf.)

Online Diet Guidance

Current Scenario

- Right now the doctor and the nurses advise the patient about his pre- and post-operation diet care.

- After the operation, the patient has to take due care about his daily diet. For this, the dietician has to guide the patients about his/her diet.

- The dietician pays a visit to the patient regularly to tell the patient about the kind of diet he has to take.

Limitations

- This activity is time consuming for the patient as well the dietician.

- The patient and the dietician have to keep track of the appointments.

Proposed Solution

When the patient wants to consult the dietician for food after and before his operation, he can do that with the help of the interactive Web site that will be built. The Web site contains a separate block for the dietician. The patient has to first log onto the site to avail the services of the dietician. Logging on is necessary because the hospital will pay the dietician for his services. In order to make sure that only the genuine patient has access to the dietician he would have to log on the Web site.

The dietician will be updating the patient's diet records and the patient can view what he has to take for the next few days. All the details will be available online. If the patient should have some queries, then he can consult the dietician online.

Advantages/Benefits

- The above changes will relieve the doctors from keeping an account of their patients' diets.

- The dietician does not have to pay a visit to the patient regularly. It will save his time.

- The patient gets rid of another kind of appointment and keeping an account of the appointment schedule.

- There would be no need to send any kind of reminders for such kind of appointment.

Issues

- A strong communication system and high speed connectivity will be required.

- A separate dietician would have to be recruited for this purpose.

The patients have to be made aware that this facility is available on the Internet and they have to be encouraged to increase the usage of the Internet services.

Hospital to Hospital Alliance

Current Scenario

- The cardiac surgeon performs operations in bigger hospitals.

- The neurologist has a basic scanning machine, but for operations she also depends on the bigger hospitals.

- The problem statement does not specify anything about the ambulance service of the hospital so we assume that the hospital does not have ambulance.

- The hospital does not have a second-tier doctor.

- There is no other specialist in the hospital.

Limitations

- Due to the unavailability of second-tier doctors emergency cases cannot be handled in the absence of the two doctors.

- Since there is no other specialist in the hospital, patients with problems connected to other causes than the heart and brain cannot be attended.

Proposed Solution

There is a need for the hospital to collaborate with the bigger hospitals not only for performing operations but also to handle emergency cases (See Emergency Case Handlings ection).

As soon as a case comes into the hospital, the staff should check with the availability of operation theatres with the bigger hospitals. This would be done if the hospital system has access to the system of the bigger hospital. In this, the system can automatically check with the schedules of the bigger hospitals. If the required conditions are available, then the system in our hospital will book the place for the patient recently admitted. If a situation arises that the operation theatre is not available, then the central system of the bigger hospital will try to make arrangements with other collaborating hospital. In this way the chain of communication and checking will continue until the search reaches some vacant operation theatre.

Right now the patients with other problems are not attended. To overcome this, doctors of other fields will also visit the hospital whenever a corresponding case turns up. The hospitals having all the specializations will be contacted if a case turns up. If the hospital is capable of attending the patient, then he will be admitted. Otherwise the bigger hospitals will be contacted as in the case of emergency and the patient will be transferred to the hospital where he can get proper treatment and attention.

Advantages/Benefits

- No patient will be turned down to the unavailability of beds and the specialist he is looking for.
- The hospital will have access to a strong network and large number of hospital facilities.

The patient will feel free to come into the hospital anytime irrespective of the type of problem he is facing.

Issues

* To acquire such network the hospital owners would have to talk to a number of hospitals and doctors.

  This idea will require the implementation of Web services.

* The launching of Web services to form the human independent network will require a look into many legal and security matters.

Hospital to Pharmacy Alliance

Current Scenario

* The hospital currently does not have any links to any pharmacy (It is not stated in the problem statement, so we assume as above).

Limitations

* One of the staff members would have to keep an account of the inventory level of the hospital.

* Due to small staff, the inventory handling will increase the staff duty.

* Since the hospital wants certain drug supplies from overseas pharmacy, this increases the diplomatic duties of the hospital and the doctors.

Proposed Solution

The inventory of the hospital will be automated so as to relieve the hospital staff of one extra duty. All the inventories in hospital will have entries in the central system. These entries will have details of the name of the medicine, its expiry date and the amount of inventory purchased.

The bottles of the medicine will have barcodes on the top. The bar codes will contain the name of the medicine and the expiry date. The place where the inventory will be kept will have sensors all over. These sensors will monitor the expiry dates of the inventory on a daily basis. When it finds a certain bottle with an expiry date near, it will automatically discard the bottle and reduce the total number of that drug by the number of bottles discarded.

This system will be linked to the some pharmacy outside the hospital (overseas or in country). When the system reaches a particular level of inventory, i.e., about to reach the finishing point of the inventory, it will send a request to the central system operator. This request will ask the user whether new inventory is to be ordered. If the response is positive, then an order will be sent to the pharmacy for the inventory needed. If that particular pharmacy does not have the drug required, then it will contact other places to fulfill the order. A chain of pharmacies will collaborate to satisfy the needs of the hospital inventory.

In a similar manner, the pharmacy will send its bill through the chain and payment will be made as soon as it reaches the operator. All this process will be accomplished through the Internet.

To pay the bill for the pharmacy, the authorization of the operator will be required. As soon as it gets the sanction of the operator, the invoice will reach the hospital bank and then make the corresponding payments.

Advantages/Benefits

- With the chain of pharmacy, not only the inventory requirements of the hospital are met, but also business-to-business alliance for the pharmacies gets facilitated.
- The staff is relieved of the inventory maintenance.
- With this kind of alliance, overseas pharmacies can also get involved and provide foreign medicines.
- It will facilitate the globalization of the Indian businesses abroad.

Issues

- To acquire such a network, the hospital owners would have to talk to a number of hospitals and doctors.
- This idea will require the implementation of Web services.
- The launching of Web services to form the human independent network will require a look into many legal and security matters.

Hospital and Other Alliances

Current Scenario

- The hospital does not have a direct links with the banks, insurance company, etc.
- The billing, payment, etc., are done in normal, routine way.

Limitations

- Due to the normal way of attending routine tasks, extra time has to be devoted to perform the job.
- The number of employees is few, so this becomes an extra effort on their part to be accomplished.
- The doctors, who are also the head of the organization, have to keep an account of the employees' monthly salaries.

Proposed Solution

The computer systems of the hospital will be linked with the bank services like the credit card facilities. With this the hospital staffs will not be bothered about the payment role. The patients can make their payment on the Internet and the amount will be automatically transferred to the hospital account. In a similar manner the patient, when setting an online account with the hospital, will not be required to enter all his personal details. Only the credit card details will be required on the patient's part. The rest of the details will be provided with the bank. This will free the patient from doing the tedious job of entering the details correctly.

When the salary of the employees will be given, the software in the hospital will calculate the amount to be given according to the shifts. This amount will then be notified to the corresponding banks of the employees. The employee's bank account will get that amount automatically and the corresponding amount will be deducted from the hospital's bank account. In this way, you get rid off keeping an account of the employee's monthly salary.

Advantages/Benefits

- Automated salary calculation is less time consuming and does not require human intervention.
- You have more time to do something more important than keeping an account of the hospital financial status.
- No cashier required for the purpose of maintaining the payments and bills of the hospital services.

Issues

- Strategic alliances have to be formed with the bank.
- Security issues have to be looked upon, as this is related to money transactions.
- Only authorized human intervention will be involved.
- Extensive use of Web services is required.

Marketing Issues

Marketing is one factor that needs careful attention during the globalization process and NSH is no exception. NSH needs to adopt its competitive marketing strategies as a promotion tool to compete with its global competitors. There are many different ways and methods that can be used to promote NSH to the people at large, as well as to partnering organizations. It is worth mentioning that the marketing of e-NSH itself will not be merely on the Internet. It will be a combination of electronic marketing, as well as physical marketing through conventional marketing channels. The following needs to be considered in marketing of e-NSH at a global level.

Combining electronic marketing with physical marketing. Therefore, handing out of business cards, NSH flyers, billboards and TV/radio advertisements can be combined with advertisements on Web sites, and promotion through friends and families.

Forming strategic alliances and partnerships with main hospitals in the region. This is an important marketing as well as expansion strategy, as NSH can use the infrastructure provided by bigger hospitals, but at the same time source patients who may be interested in the personalized services offered by e-NSH.

Connection with doctors and medical experts from other hospitals. This is very helpful in the medical profession where not all expertise would reside with an individual doctor. In case of NSH, there should be consideration given to, and recognition of, other medical experts, especially from different specializations. NSH may use video-conferencing functionalities to communicate and consult with other medical experts, especially in the areas that NSH is not an expert in. In this way, they could treat patients more effectively. For example, when patients are facing problems other than heart or brain, they could recommend other doctors that are more appropriate in other clinics or hospitals. On the other hand, if other patients in other clinics or hospitals are facing cardiac problems, the doctors could recommend them to NSH.

The gregarious nature of e-NSH owner-doctors could be used, through participation in socio-cultural activities (such as the Rotary) to promote the "good values" of their hospital. E-NSH may also participate in sponsorships and donations for worthwhile causes, resulting from the globalization process.

Conducting joint research with other hospitals is another marketing tool. NSH can gain recognition and reputation by joining in medical research with other hospitals. As mentioned above, meeting people of status and influence could greatly assist NSH. Also, getting involved in the research for cures against specific illnesses and diseases can greatly help them in gaining trust and recognition from the community.

Providing graduate training for medical students as well as offering university sponsorship can be a way to gain reputation and acceptance from the community. We all know that the new generation will be the assets of the future, and exposure to them is a huge marketing prospect. Medical students will need to have working experience and NSH could provide such facilities to them. NSH could even go to the extent to provide sponsorships to medical student Network Architecture.

Global Team Management

NSH could ask why they need to outsource. Outsourcing is preferred, as NSH does not have such departments to do the jobs. In order to set-up these departments, it will mean that the cost will rise dramatically. Outsourcing can provide significant savings and an opportunity for an e-business to focus on its core competencies. Outsourcing can help to be cost effective, as NSH does not need to worry about hiring the right people or to train employees to do their jobs. However, the management of outsourcing vendors can be one of the more challenging aspects of running an e-business.

A survey conducted by PriceWaterHouseCoopers reports that only 55% of executives surveyed described their outsource relationships as "successful." (PWC, 2000) NSH should be aware from the result of the survey that the main difficulties encountered were managing scope, managing vendor operations, obtaining adequate skills, and agreeing on standards of excellence.

Outsourcing can provide significant savings and an opportunity for an e-business to focus on its core competencies. A recent survey indicated most organizations seeking technology suppliers are more interested in high quality support and strong relationships than technical leadership and price (Grayson, 2002). The ability to be responsive and add value to a relationship is among the important attributes that NSH should take note of when selecting a long-term IT provider.

However, the management of outsourcing vendors can be one of the more challenging aspects of running an e-business. Despite the view that outsourcing offers cost effectiveness and improves flexibility, it also has its dark side when it comes to industry structure.

As competitors turn to the same vendors, the project development may become more homogeneous. Thus, it may erode a company's distinctiveness and cause price competition against competitors.

Moreover, outsourcing lowers barriers of entry because a new entrant need only assemble purchased inputs.

In addition, companies lose control over important elements of their business, and crucial experience shifts to suppliers, thus enhancing their power in the long run.

These views are emphasized by a recent survey whereby there were growing frustrations among corporate users with information technology outsourcing on the issues of escalating costs and failure to deliver promised results (Chong, 2002). Some IT vendors persuade companies to upgrade their IT platforms, even when they do not need to, which is costly and would not support previous versions.

In conclusion, the success or failure of an outsourcing arrangement depends upon more than just the choice of outsourcing vendors and contract provisions.

It is imperative for NSH's management that thoughtful planning of the transition process, and careful management of the vendor once that transition has taken place, will help ensure that an e-business venture would reap the full benefits of outsourcing.

While the exact outsourcing vendor is not specified here, it would not unusual to outsource the development and testing of the IT solution to software shops specializing in this work in well-known IT centers in India, Indonesia, Israel or Ireland. MS consulting, though, will have to continue to monitor the progress of the outsourced company and ensure that it is meeting the objectives of NSH. It should also be mentioned that even during the development of IT solutions, when it comes to global teams, some aspects of the globalization process come into play. For example, it becomes essential to consider the location and time difference of team members dealing with the development process. Examples of groupware technologies, as discussed in Chapter V, are invaluable in managing development teams, and the now ubiquitous tools of chat rooms, e-mails, telephone calls, and short message services (SMS) can be used to maintain ongoing good communication. Constant communication can help in correcting and supervising the project. Using chat rooms and e-communications can help in keeping the costs of communications down.

Applying Technology GET

In addition to the hardware and software used for the Web servers, database servers, internal systems and external infrastructure, an important consideration is the standard for medical information interchange - Health Level 7 (HL7).

HL7 is a standard for information exchange between medical applications environment. HL7 is called "Level Seven" because its message formats are layered upon the seventh level of the Open Systems Interconnection (OSI) protocol of the International Standards Organization (ISO).

There are several reasons why we have decided to adopt this standard. The most obvious reason is that having a common message protocol minimizes the number of interfaces that are needed to integrate with other systems. This would be imperative in the case of our alliances, upon which most of our solutions are based. This also helps reduce the time taken for development and implementation.

Another consideration in implementing the mobile solutions will be the technology used and its impact on the patient's health. As we deal with patients who might have pacemakers and other similar devices implanted in their bodies, the technology used for mobile communications must be proven as safe before deployment.

The next sections describe the proposed system in the following areas:

- NSH Web site map.
- Database and software components.
- Hardware components.
- Mobile technology.
- Security.

Figure 6.2. NSH Web site map

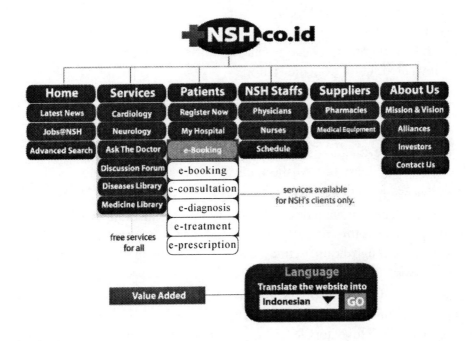

NSH Web Site Map

The proposed NSH Web site will be registered as www.nsh.co.id. There are six sections, which are called Home, Services, Patients, NSH Staffs, Suppliers and About Us (the blue text boxes as in the Figure 6.2).

Home will be accessed as the main page from NSH Web site. This section can be accessed by all visitors and only contains general information such as medical news, latest research and development in related health care services, job opportunities and a search engine within the NSH site and the whole Web.

The second section is called Services. Basically, it provides information on the NSH health care areas, cardiology and neurology. In addition, this section also offers free services for the community through Ask the Doctor, Discussion Forum and Encyclopedia in Diseases and Medicine terms. Ask the Doctor is a question-asked session which is accompanied by answers provided by an NSH doctor. Discussion Forum covers many health care topics. Visitors can join or contribute his/her opinion and share their views with others. The diseases and medicine encyclopedia can be used for knowledge sharing. All visitors can visit Services section.

Next is Patients section, which is only accessible by NSH's members. To become a member is easy. One only needs to first simply fill in registration form then read NSH's terms and conditions of use, privacy policy and security policy agreements. Once a visitor agrees with all the conditions, then that person is now an NSH member. The terms and conditions can legally save NSH from any unwanted action from the visitors.

Every member will have personalized page, which is called My Hospital. In here, the member can change or modify their preferences, such as address details. In addition, all NSH members can have access to online booking, e-consultation, e-diagnosis, e-treatment and e-prescription (the orange text boxes as in the Figure 14). All the medical services mentioned previously come with charges depending on the technology involved (e.g., video-conferencing).

The fourth section is named NSH Staffs, simply because only authorized NSH staffs can access this site. Physicians and nurses are now enabled to work effectively through the use of Internet and NSH Web site. This section provides staffs' roster and, moreover, access for patients' records.

The proposed Web site also supports direct connection to suppliers (e.g., pharmacies and medical equipment suppliers). The link to pharmacies can minimize NSH's inventory level, however the most important advantage is that collaboration provides efficiency in ordering and receiving medical supplies. As a result, this site can only be accessed by an authorized party.

The last section is called About Us, this page contains general information about NSH hospital, its mission and vision statements, strategic alliances, investor-related and other contact details. All visitors are free to browse this section.

The proposed Web site will be created in Multilanguage, which can be called value added. The objective is to attract more and more visitors and also to provide an ease for the users.

Database and Software Components

Database Requirements

For NSH, data availability is an important issue for the success of e-hospital. The proposed database system should be reliable, scalable, secure and cost effective. The data should be available 24/7 for physicians, nurses and patients. All chosen database components including hardware and software should be reliable in supporting NSH health care services and have the ability to serve high data enquiries. Data security is another important issue, as the database design must ensure that only authorized parties can access or modify the data. The last issue is about data storage. NSH health care services are dealing with multimedia files (voice, text, data, image and video), therefore an effective storage is required.

Software Components

NSH accounting software is needed to deal with the customer billing, financial information and taxation purpose. The accounting software is mainly designed for distribution-oriented businesses that require sophisticated accounting functions and a powerful inventory control system. It contains many advanced features such as three styles of invoicing (service, distribution and recurrent), multi-currency capabilities, multiple bank account capabilities, multi-warehouse inventory control and other advanced features. A typical accounting system that can be upgraded to multiple users, and that will include General Ledger, Accounts Receivable, Accounts Payable, Inventory, Distribution

Invoicing, Purchase Orders, Sales Statistics and Purchasing Statistics is suggested here.

The computerized or electronic record is defined as a paperless patient chart and is often referred to by varying terms, the Computerized Patient Record (CPR), the Electronic Medical Record (EMR) or the Electronic Patient Record (EPR). There are five levels of complexity encompassing the paperless charts and corresponding to the level of implementation.

Firstly, automated medical reports are in the paper format and computerized to the point where specific automated tasks can be conducted. Second level, records are handwritten, dictated or transcribed and indexed or scanned into an electronic system that offers the same functions as a paper-based system. It is recording the health care process and providing accessibility to previously recorded information.

The third level is EMR, an upgraded version of these reports. It contains the same scope of information and the information is arranged for computer use. It also typically contains document imaging and interfaces to core components of care delivery such as ordering and retrieving laboratory tests, prescription writing, consultation or referral notes, and billing. Fourthly, CPR focuses on the patient and contains information from one or more provider enterprises. The CPR combines several medical records concerning one patient and assembles a record that goes beyond the enterprise-based retention period.

In addition, the final level is the electronic health record. It is a more comprehensive collection of the individual's or patient's health information. This level includes a network of provider and non-provider settings based on the patient's health and wellness. This level requires an information infrastructure that involves homes, providers and other sites.

NSH will use the Smart Clinic software to keep and record the patient medical report. Smart Clinic is an easily used customer-based patient record that enhances medical record documentation and reimbursement capabilities for the doctor to focus on the patient.

Smart Clinic allows for various staff entries for the physician, office staff, or hospitals, and allows for mobile access to all patient information, when you are on-call at home or doing hospital rounds. The system "thinks" like a doctor and flows to accommodate the physician's actual workflow.

Smart-Series products have been designed by doctors for doctors to automate the entire spectrum of clinical activities from patient history, review of systems and physical exam, progress notes, prescriptions, tests, orders and delivery of results directly to your computer. The doctor will see more patients in less time, allowing more time for those faces waiting at home.

In the traditional method, the rostering system will become a more time consuming, frustrating task, and unexpected errors will arise. The cost of maintaining a roster can be very expensive and inaccuracies with roster shift will rise from the frustrated staff.

Digital Instinct provides the software called Virtual Roster Enterprise. The software is developed and designed to suit the most complicated roster. Virtual Roster uses advanced algorithms to analyze, optimize and roster, based on specified requirements. The software has been developed with large scale operations, such as hospitals and casinos.

Using Virtual Roster will reduce the administration cost and increase productivity. The software used to create roster automatically assigns the staff or employee to the specific tasks.

Hardware Components

Hardware Infrastructure for the Waiting Room

An interactive kiosk will be placed in the waiting room. The workstation is accessible by all users in the hospital, however its operating system should only be available by NSH's staff. The kiosk provides general information about the hospital and pertinent medical materials. The application will be either used as a highly restricted, Web-enabled system or a stand-alone application. The kiosk's interface consists of touch screen, optical mouse and keyboard for interaction.

After evaluating different kiosks, MS Consulting decided to implement Sparc kiosk from Abuzz Technologies, one of the leading kiosk manufacturers in Sydney, Australia (http://www.mediatec.ie/htmlsite/ts_sparc_kiosk.htm). The sleek Sparc kiosk is suitable for public access and a wide range of applications, including hospital settings. Sparc kiosk is elegantly design with 15" NEC touch screen and curved aluminum sides.

In addition to kiosk, 42" Sony plasma wide screen is presented in the waiting room for small audiences of one to 20 people. The plasma display will be used to provide short medical videos or information news to entertain the hospital's audiences. A Sony recorder/player is also added in the waiting room to accompany the plasma display.

Hardware Infrastructure for the Examination Rooms

The computing equipment in the exam rooms should be fitted into a small room. After performing market research, MethodScience Consulting proposes OptiPlex SX260, the smallest desktop PC from Dell, as the workstation for the exam rooms. The OptiPlex SX260 chassis supports mounting options, for example wall mount brackets.

Dell is known as one of the leading computer manufacturers for its technology, performance and value. Dell OptiPlex series are suitable for networked environments and are moreover reliable, easy to manage and support demanding applications. In addition, Dell offers affordable prices and provides technical support.

Hardware Infrastructure for the Physician Rooms

Every physician room will be equipped with computing facilities and the solution falls to Dell ultimate notebook, Inspiron 8500. MethodScience Consulting proposes notebooks instead of desktop PCs because of the mobility factor. The machine itself is as powerful as a performance desktop with a 15-inch display. Physicians could bring their notebook on remote duties for efficiency in medical services.

Hardware Infrastructure for the Nurse Workstations

The nurse workstations should be more powerful and distinct from the computers located in the waiting and exam rooms. The workstation should allow a wide range of programs like digital images and Electronic Medical Record. Performance desktop, Dell Dimension 8250 will be used to help nurses with their tasks. With the Intel Pentium 4 processor, Dell Dimension 8250 supports fast and powerful access to multimedia and Internet technologies.

Hardware Infrastructure for the Staff Workstations

The staff workstation is used by a receptionist for basic administration operations such as patient's booking time, appointments, charges and others. Again, MethodScience Consulting recommends one of Dell products, Dimension 2350 which is a very affordable computer for essential computing and fully supported with Dell's customer service. In addition, a multifunction device (printer, scanner, copier and fax machine) is added to support business operations. MethodScience Consulting suggests the purchase of the HP LaserJet 3300mfp.

Networking Architecture

Network infrastructure is built to provide a robust and reliable system which enables access to the NSH Web site from remote locations and provide high connectivity audio and video through adequate bandwidth. Virtual Private Network (VPN) is used for connection with other hospital alliances. Wide Area Network (WAN) provides global communication and connectivity between users. Local Area Network (LAN) supports local communication within the NSH hospital. The design should be flexible for future expansion without affecting major impacts on the present system and allow easy updates to the infrastructure.

Mobile Technology

The use of mobile technology in the health care services shows promising signs. In fact, handheld devices like Personal Digital Assistants (PDAs), tablets and smart cellular phones can provide better decision support at point-of-care. According to Advisory Board, 67% physicians are now using handheld devices. The implementation of mobile technology provides advantages for physicians, nurses, patients and suppliers.

Physicians

Mobile technology can increase a physician's productivity, improve health care services to patients and eliminate geographical distances. The example of mobile technology which is designed for physicians is TouchWorks from Allscripts Healthcare Solutions (http://www.allscripts.com/ahcs/solutions_fs.htm).

In addition, physicians also use mobile technology for:

- Mobility – Conducting conference calls with nurses in case there is any emergency in the hospital when a physician is not in the hospital.
- Fast access to patient records.
- Reduce paper-based systems.

Nurses

The use of mobile technology is not only focused for physicians. Today's nurses also carry handheld devices to support their tasks. The mobile technology benefits for nurses:

- Provide immediate access to patient information.
- Transmit data into Electronic Patient Records (ERP).
- Provide efficient and better health care services for patients.
- Enable conference calls with physician for medical treatment.
- Check schedule.

Patients

NSH is a health care provider specialized in cardiac and neuro diseases. The use of mobile technology has given greater flexibility for the patients without being required to physically go to the hospital for a check up. There are many types of medical equipment that can be used by outpatients. One of the examples is CareLink (cardiac device) from Medtronic.

Another example is the combination between mobile phones and remote cardiac devices which enable a physician to check the heart activity of the patient. The device is designed by Lucent Technologies' Bell Labs.

One of the products from SmartMeds.com will enable to provide services for patients who are using handheld device. The services offered include scheduling for medication, any medical news and refilling prescriptions.

Suppliers (e.g., Pharmacies)

Mobile technology improves receiving and ordering processes between the hospital and its drug suppliers. In addition, it also provides better management and storage systems. Mobile Solutions from Cardinal Health is a handheld device which is equipped with scanning device based on Pocket PC. This device enables NSH's staff to work directly with hospital inventory. Simply face the bar code of the product into the device then all the details will be displayed. This can result in efficiency for ordering purpose.

Security Policies

Access Security

NSH security policy must incorporate acceptable use of networks and computers in the elsewhere. For instance, password policy will determine how passwords are created, how often they are reviewed and how frequently they should be changed. Lawrence (2002) stated that only an acceptable and fully understandable policy on e-mail use should be instituted.

Firewall Security

The purpose of the firewall is to protect the bank's internal network from outside observation and intruders. It provides SFNB (Security First Network Bank) protection from outside obstruction. There will be additional barriers between the Internet and the internal bank network. Firewalls provide filtering routers to examine any information that is sent across the Internet through the customer service network.

All traffic passing the firewall is filtered by an e-mail proxy, and it will eliminate any with suspicious attachments or subject lines. The proxy then changes the IP address of the packet to deliver it to the appropriate site within the internal network. This protects inside addresses from outside access (Kalakota & Whinston, 1997).

Access and Authorization

Authentication is a process to control access and resources. It must be able to identify the users. The process might involve the method of using user name and password to token-based technologies and digital certificates.

The next process is authorization, where the users are authenticated. The security solution should define and control exactly which resources they are allowed to use. NSH needs to ensure the security infrastructure is implemented. In order to protect patients' or customers' information, NSH must maintain physical security of the servers and control access to software passwords and private keys.

Security is enhanced with entire transaction travels under the protection of public-key encryption, with the digital certificate verifying the purchaser's identity, the digital wallet hiding the card data, and the encryption rendering the transaction difficult to hack (Randall, 2002). Typically, the requirement to support wireless access involves adding large numbers of new devices to the environment, and the infrastructure must be able to handle it.

Digital Signature

Digital signature is a security system which uses a public cryptography system or it also can be defined as a data value generated by a public key algorithm based on the contents of a lock data and a private key, yielding so individualized crypto checksum (Wibowo, 1999).

Legal Issues

NSH needs to maintain the important trust relationship within their electronic business partners, clients and subscribers. The aims and purposes are to ensure the integrity and security of the data are maintained for the purposes of risk management and dispute resolution (Lawrence et al., 2002). NSH needs to be aware of the legal environment in the country of its operation, as well as from where its patients will be accessing the information. Legal issues encompass issues such as privacy, taxation, copyright and a whole series of other issues that have acquired a new importance due to the digital revolution in order to build up e-confidence toward the stakeholders (Rotenberg, 2001).

Intellectual Property

The purpose is to create a balance between the protection of rights for copyright owners and increased public access to intellectual property. NSH needs to comply with intellectual and copyright laws and any new development in this area which will include knowledge and information expertise.

Taxation

There are two main areas on the taxation, which are income tax and good and services taxes in most countries. It is therefore essential for e-NSH to comply with the taxation issues of relevant countries.

Consumer Protection Law

Consumer can be defined as any person who uses any goods or services available to the public, either for a person's own or his/her family's interests, for other persons and living creatures, but not for trade.

According to the Law no: 8 1999 (Gingerich and Teo, 2001) that it sets out very specifically the rights and obligations for both consumers and business players. However, it places more emphasis on the rights of Consumers and the obligations of business players.

The rights of consumers include the right:

- To enjoy security and safety in consuming goods or services (e.g., the products must contain expiry dates).

- To select and to obtain any goods or services in accordance with their exchange value and the condition and security promised (for example, public facilities such as water and electricity are currently monopolized by state-owned companies, so that consumers have no option then to buy the facilities from them).

- To obtain accurate, clear and honest information on goods or services which means that advertisements must give true and correct information on the products.

- To have their opinions and complaints about goods or services heard (e.g., business players must accept complaints from their customers relating to their products).

- To obtain appropriate support, protection and effort to settle disputes over the protection of consumers.

- To obtain guidance and education on consumers' rights (e.g., information on goods or services).

- To be treated or served fairly and honestly, without discrimination.

- To obtain compensation for loss, if the goods and/or services received are not in accordance with the agreement or are not appropriate.

- The obligations of the business players include the duty (http://www.dprin.go.id/indonesia/bisnis/default.asp).

- To act in good faith when carrying on their business.

- To provide correct, clear and honest information on the condition and security of the goods or services, and to explain their use, repair and maintenance.

- To treat or serve consumers politely, honestly and without discrimination;

- To guarantee the quality of the goods and/or services provided and/or traded, according to the applicable quality standard of the goods and/or services.

- To give consumers a chance to test goods and/or certain services, and to guarantee any goods manufactured and/or traded;

- To compensate for any loss suffered arising from the use of any traded goods and/or services.
- To compensate for any loss, if the goods and/or services received or being need are not in accordance with any agreement.

Cost Analysis

Rapid Return on Investment

The payback function of business process metrics such as frequency, volume, effort level and the level of improvement can be gained by comparing the existing process and future process. It is expected the implementation perspective and the complexity of automating the process should be factored in as well where more complex routing and approval are required. In order to determine the implementation, priorities should be established and the project team must assess the value proposition of each individual process. It also might include the ability to implement the faster solution component.

Additional informational processes related to benefits, leave, personnel policies, job postings and payroll data should also be considered as part of a rapid ROI strategy. Due to these self-services, the projects can be implemented quickly. In fact, NSH starts with information-based employee self-service before moving forward with input-based processes. These projects are expected to improve customer service and employee self-sufficiency.

Cost and Benefit Analysis

The implementation of e-business strategy and infrastructure reform in NSH is expected to have a growth in services, market position and cost reduction in the long term. The projected cost and benefit analysis might lead to a beneficial and viable project.

Table 6.3. Strategic and transition cost

Estimated Strategic Cost	Estimated Strategic and Transition Cost
Breakdown of Total Investment Cost	$835,000
Strategic Assessment	$200,000
Marketing	$110,000
Software Development	$320,000
Total	$630,000
Estimated Transition Cost	
Technology	
Servers	$60,000
Firewall	$45,000
Switch	$5,000
Routers	$15,000
Workstations	$50,000
Training	$60,000
Total	$235,000

Strategic and Transition Costs

Based on the research, the estimated cost of initial e-business investment is about $835,000 as shown in Table 6.3. The estimated strategic cost is divided into three parts: strategic assessment, marketing and software development. Strategic cost will include some business association (alliance) cost and e-business cost. Whereas software development will lead to the changes or updating the software used in the certain period of time (virtual roster, accounting software, etc.). The estimated strategic cost will add up to be around $630,000.

Another projection is on the transition cost, where it is estimated around $235,000 to spend on the technology and training. The technology is important for a hospital to increase the efficiency and effectiveness of its business activities. The estimation is supported by the projected operating cost spread over a three-year period in the next section.

Training of staff apart from the change management process is required to be implemented. It is one necessary factor to consider due to the changes of recent technology. This might assist the NSH staff as it moves into the next level of the global information development. The estimated cost is around $60,000.

Table 6.4. Profit and loss statement forecast

Profit and Loss Statement Forecast	Projected Operating Cost		
	Year 1	Year 2	Year 3
Revenue	$ 1,350,000	$ 1,500,000	$ 2,010,000
Total Revenue	$ 1,350,000	$ 1,500,000	$ 2,010,000
Expenses:			
Advertising and Promotion	$ 130,000	$ 100,000	$ 70,000
System Maintenance	$ 200,000	$ 160,000	$ 115,000
Call Centre	$ 20,000	$ 20,000	$ 20,000
Total Cost	$ 350,000	$ 280,000	$ 205,000
Net Profit	$ 1,000,000	$ 1,220,000	$ 1,805,000
Assumptions: 1. Local inflation rate 10% 2. Interest rate 12%			
	Year 1	Year 2	Year 3
Projected Revenue Growth	14%	16%	24%
Global Market Share	5.4%	5.5%	5.8%
Gross Profit Margin	21.0%	24.0%	26.0%
Profit Margin (After Tax)	10.2%	10.5%	10.7%

Projected Operating Costs

NSH's three-year financial forecast analysis was used to estimate profitability or losses that might be incurred during the course of the transition. It is estimated that NSH would start to realize the benefits gain from investing in the first year. It is expected to have a growth rate around 14% in the year and continue to rise gradually in the second year and third year.

The inflation rate for a typical developing nation is assumed at a high 10%. In this case study, we have assumed this rate with knowledge that in real life it will usually be much less than this. However, readers should be aware of factoring some inflation in their calculations. As a result, high inflation in the country that is home to NSH is set positive to increase the revenue constantly. In addition the interest rate is around 12%, therefore the expected revenue growth will be higher than the interest rate. It is important to have positive objectives in the projected profit and loss statement to attract more investors into the project.

Conclusion

In this chapter, we applied the concepts of Global Enterprise Transitions, as discussed in the previous five chapters of this book, to a hypothetical North-South Hospital (NSH), which is based on a real small to medium hospital in one of the developing nations. NSH was described as a small hospital with only ten beds, having numerous limitations that are meant to be handled by the application of GET. The two owner-doctors are shown as moving their hospital to e-NSH, thereby providing access to patients globally, as well as handling their own challenges in terms of not being consumed by mundane tasks. Instead, with e-NSH, they will be able to have their own personal time, and also provide excellent quality service to their patients. The strategy outlined here will grow the hospital as well, providing returns in terms of financial rewards to the skilled owners.

An all-inclusive networking topology, strategic applications and systems are in place to realize e-business transition of NSH. The networking topology will facilitate the e-transformation of NSH into a networked e-business, as aimed for with GET.

The cost and benefit analysis has also shown a strong return on investment (ROI) for the proposed globalization solution. The projected revenue growth and profit margin is showing a steady growth, making this project a profitable one for the owners. As stated in our SWOT analysis, the initial weakness of investment costs can be easily offset with successful implementation of GET. Considering the projected graph of ROI, we can see that there is a strong prospect for profit, with a break–even point appearing in one and a half years.

In conclusion, the GET process forms the backbone of transitioning the hospital to a global hospital utilizing the communications technologies.

References

Adnan, M. (2003). Retrieved June 14, 2003 from the World Wide Web at: *http://www.geocities.com/amwibowo/resource/hukum/hukum_eb.pdf*

Asia Pacific-wide connectivity for Nokia. (2003). Retrieved June 14, 2003 from the World Wide Web at: *http://business.singtel.com/upload_hub/mnc/nokia-grp.pdf*

Baldwin, A., Beres, Y., Mont, M.C., & Shiu, S. (2001). Trust service: A trust infrastructure for e-commerce. Hewlett-Packard Corporation. Retrieved June 14, 2003 from the World Wide Web at: *http://www.hpl.hp.com/techreports/2001/HPL-2001-198.pdf*

Barrell, Alan W. (1991). *Building A global business*. Director Books.

Campbell, C.M. (2001, October 15). Think customer satisfaction, not cost savings, when going wireless. *CRM Tips & Newsletters*. Retrieved from the World Wide Web at: *http://searchcrm.techtarget.com/tip/1,289483,sid11_gci776662,00.html*

Chong, F. (2002, April 2). Corporate backlash against IT. *The Australian IT*. Available: *http://ww.australianit.com.au*

Cisco 7200 Series Router. Retrieved June 14, 2003 from the World Wide Web at: *http://www.cisco.com/en/US/products/hw/routers/ps341/index.htm*

Cisco Catalyst 8500 Series Multiservice Switch Routers. Retrieved from the World Wide Web at: *http://www.cisco.com/en/US/products/hw/switches/ps718/index.html*

Cisco PIX 500 Series Firewalls. Retrieved from the World Wide Web at: *http://www.cisco.com/en/US/products/hw/vpndevc/ps2030/index.htm*

Deitel, H. M., Deitel, P. J., & Steinbuhler, K. (2001). *E-business and e-commerce for managers*. New York: Prentice Hall.

Dell Dimension 2350, 8250, Inspirion 8500, OptiPlex SX260, PowerEdge 6650, PowerVault 112T and other suggested hardware. Retrieved June 28, 2004 from the World Wide Web at: *http://www.ap.dell.com/ap/au/en/bsd/products/*

Ghoshal, S., & Bartlett, C.A. (1997). *The individualized corporation*. New York: Harper Business.

Gingerich., D., & Teo., C. (2001). E-commerce legal guide. Retrieved June 14, 2003 from the World Wide Web at: *http://www.bakerinfo.com/apec/indoapec_main.htm#1.3*

Grayson, I. (2002, March 19). Support is tops, not price. *The Australian IT*. Retrieved from the World Wide Web at: *http://ww.australianit.com.au*

Grime, B. (2002, December/January). Making the most of CRM. *Information Age*, 22-27.

How CareLink Works. (2003). Retrieved June 14, 2003 from the World Wide Web at: *http://www.medtronic.com/carelink/features.html*

India Telemedicine. (2004). Retrieved April 23, 2004 from the World Wide Web at: *http://www.indiatelemedicine.com/telemedtech.shtml*

Kalakota, R., & Whinston, A.B. (1997). *Electronic commerce: A manager's guide*. Addison Wesley Longman.

Lawrence, E., Newton, S., Corbitt, B., Braithwaite, R., & Parker, C. (2002). *Technology of Internet business*. John Wiley & Sons Australia.

Low, S. (2001). The British Chambers of Commerce manifesto for e-business. Retrieved June 14, 2003 from the World Wide Web at: *http://www.britishchambers.org.uk/newsandpolicy/ict/ebusinessmn.htm*

Malhorta, Y. (1998). Business process redesign: An overview. *IEEE Engineering Management Review, 26*(3).

Medcon – Telemedicine technology. Retrieved April 23, 2003 from the World Wide Web at: *http://www.medcon.com/*

Medical Record Institute. (2003). Retrieved April 18, 2003 from the World Wide Web at: *http://www.medrecinst.com/conferences/tepr/*

Mobile health vare to link providers, patients. (2000, November 9). Retrieved June 14, 2003 from the World Wide Web at: *http://www.newsfactor.com/perl/story/4789.html*

Mobile phone tracks heartbeats. (2002, December 14). Retrieved June 14, 2003 from the World Wide Web at: *http://news.bbc.co.uk/1/hi/technology/2562265.stm*

Mobile dolutions from cardinal health. (2003).Retrieved June 14, 2003 from the World Wide Web at: *http://www.cardinal.com/content/pharmacies/hospital/phhodsinvmantech.asp*

Mobileinfo.com. (2002). Wireless CRM. Retrieved from the World Wide Web at: *http://www.mobileinfo.com/Hot_topics/Wireless_CRM.htm*

Oracle9i Database. (2003). Product Editions Retrieved June 14, 2003 from the World Wide Web at: *http://www.oracle.com/ip/deploy/database/oracle9i/index.html?oracle9idb_features2.html*

Ostermann, D. (2001). *Executive agenda: Ideas and insights for business, 4*(1) Second Quarter.

PWC. (2000). Directions in IT outsourcing.

Raharjo, B. (1999). Retrieved June 14, 2003 from the World Wide Web at: *http://budi.insan.co.id/articles/1999-02.pdf*

Raskino, M. (2001, November). Directing e-business at Intel: Transforming a corporation. *Gartner Research.* Retrieved from the World Wide Web at: *http://www4.gartner.com*

Rotenberg, M. (2001). Confidence and e-commerce. Retrieved June 14, 2003 from the World Wide Web at: *http://www.oecdobserve.org/ news/printpage.php/aid/409/Confidence and_e-commerce.html*

Songini, M. (2001, October 5). Wireless CRM: Strings. *ComputerWorld.*

The Association of Telehealth Service Providers (ATSP). (2003). Retrieved April 18, 2003 from the World Wide Web at: *http://www.atsp.org/ telemedicine/homepage.asp*

Tivoli. (2000). Securing e-business. IBM Corporation. Retrieved June 14, 2003 from the World Wide Web at: *http://www.itpapers.com/techguide/ secebus.pdf*

TouchWorks. (2003). Allscripts Healthcare Solutions. Retrieved June 14, 2003 from the World Wide Web at: *http://www.allscripts.com/ahcs/ solutions_fs.htm*

Using handheld devices to obtain physicians adoption of IT. (2003). Retrieved June 14, 2003 from the World Wide Web at: *http://www.medrecinst.com/ conferences/tepr/2003/program/sessionDetail. asp?FUNC_ID=401&EVT_ID=5019&conference=MHC& PARENT_FUNC_ID=119*

Glossary

The globalization process is fraught with large number of jargons and terminologies. Although here, we do not plan to sort out the discussions completely, it will be of great assistance to our readers, if we clarify the terms as used by us in the remainder of this book.

Company, Enterprise, Firm and Organization – All four terms are used interchangeably throughout the book. They are applied to any business entity formed by a group of people with a common commercial purpose to acquire profit by means of commercial enterprise.

Framework – Refers to a structure composed of stages that fit together.

GIS (Global Information Systems) – Software systems and applications that deal with the process of globalization.

GISM (Global Information Systems Management) Activities – Activities related to the global transition process in managing information systems.

Globalization – A specific business strategy that considers the world as a single entity by using standardized products or services to approach the market.

MNC (Multinational Corporation) – Refers to a company engaged in business operations through its own affiliates in a number of countries or regions, and it manages from a global perspective

NSH (North-South Hospital) – A hypothetical hospital based on a small to medium hospital in a developing country.

Organizational Structure – It focuses on the multinational corporation's organizational structure in this study. It refers to a company's organizational characteristics in terms of configuration of assets and capabilities, roles of overseas operations, and development and diffusion of knowledge.

Transition – Refers to a passage from one position, state, or stage to another.

About the Authors

Dr. Yi-chen Lan is a senior lecturer in the School of Computing and Information Technology at the University of Western Sydney in Australia. He holds a Bachelor of Commerce – Computing and Information Systems (Honours) degree and a Ph.D. in the area of global transitions. Dr. Lan teaches information systems and management courses in both undergraduate and graduate levels. Prior to his current academic work, Dr. Lan worked in industry for five years, wherein he held senior management responsibilities in the areas of information systems and quality assurance programs in a multinational organization. His main areas of research include global transition process, global information systems management issues, globalization framework development, integrated supply chain development, and health related information systems development and management. Dr. Lan is a member of the Australian Computer Society (MACS).

Dr. Bhuvan Unhelkar has 23 years of strategic as well as hands-on professional experience in information technology, followed by three years of full-time academic experience at the University of Western Sydney in Australia. Earlier, he created and taught the subject of global information systems at the University of Technology, Sydney. He is an internationally acclaimed consultant and trainer and founding principal of MethodScience.com, specializing in the field of software processes, modeling and quality. Dr. Unhelkar has authored seven books, published numerous papers and has presented at and chaired seminars and conferences. As a senior manager with Dow Jones, he won the Computerworld Object Developers Award, for *Best Use of Object-Orientation Across the Organization.* He leads the Mobile Internet Research and Applications Group (MIRAG - Emerging Technologies sub-group) within the University of Western Sydney. Dr. Unhelkar is fellow of the Australian Computer Society (FACS), convener of the Object-Oriented Special Interest Group, and branch executive committee member of the ACS NSW branch. He is also Rotarian St.Ives (Dist. 9680), mentor director at TiE.org Sydney chapter; Friend of Chase Alive (FOCAL).

Dr. Mahesh S. Raisinghani, is a faculty member at the Graduate School of Management, Texas Woman's University in the U.S., where he teaches M.B.A. courses in information systems and e-business. He was the recipient of the 1999 UD Presidential Award, has published in numerous leading scholarly and practitioner journals, presented at leading world-level scholarly conferences and has served as an editor of three books. Dr. Raisinghani is included in the millennium edition of *Who's Who in the World, Who's Who Among America's Teachers* and *Who's Who in Information Technology.*

Index